Thoreau's Garden

Thoreau's Garden

Native Plants for the American Landscape

Peter Loewer

STACKPOLE
BOOKS

Copyright © 1996 by Peter Loewer
Published by
Stackpole Books
5067 Ritter Road
Mechanicsburg, PA 17055

Printed in the United States of America

10 9 8 7 6 5 4 3 2 1

Library of Congress Cataloging-in-Publication Data

Loewer, H. Peter.
    Thoreau's garden : native plants for the American landscape / Peter Loewer.
        p.   cm.
    ISBN 0-8117-1728-3
    1. Native plants for cultivation—United States.   2. Thoreau, Henry David,
1817–1862—Knowledge—Botany.   3. Botany—Massachusetts—Concord
Region.   I. Thoreau, Henry David, 1817–1862. Journal. Selections. II. Title.
SB439.L63   1996
635.9′517—dc20
                                                                                        96-17648
                                                                                        CIP

CONTENTS

Beware of all enterprises that require new clothes.

Henry David Thoreau, Walden, *1854*

PREFACE

SOMETIME DURING THE SUMMER OF 1968, I PURCHASED THE TWO-volume set of *The Journal of Henry D. Thoreau* from a bookstore in Manhattan. I bought the journal because my wife and I were planning to leave the city and move to an old, abandoned farm in upstate New York. We were ready to blaze a trail to another life, one closer to nature—or at least away from the nature of cities.

The edition I bought, published in 1962 by Dover Publications of New York, consists of an unabridged republication of the work that first appeared under the imprint of the Houghton Mifflin Company in 1906. This 1906 edition originally appeared in a fourteen-volume set, but to reduce the contents to two volumes Dover made new offset plates, and thus four pages were reprinted on one page.

The first extensive publication of the journal began in 1881 with *Early Spring in Massachusetts,* a volume containing extracts from the month of March and parts of February and April. It was edited by Thoreau's friend Mr. Harrison G. O. Blake, to whom the journal was bequeathed by Miss Sophia Thoreau, Henry's sister, when she died in 1876. Mr. Blake then published parts of the journal, continuing with *Summer* in 1884, *Winter* in 1887, and *Autumn* in 1892. After Mr. Blake died, the journal became the property of Mr. E. H. Russell of Worcester, who made the first effort to bring the entire contents to the reading public. The editors were Bradford Torrey and Francis H. Allen, and in addition to all sorts of brilliant editing feats—Thoreau's labored handwriting was described as strong, rapid, and none too legible, containing little, if any, punctuation—they produced one of the most polished indexes in any work I've ever consulted.

From the first entry, "'A stir is on the Worcester hills,' verse, **1,** 122" (boldface indicates volume number), to the last entry, "Zoroaster, **1,** 371," this index is such a marvel of scholarship that it may embarrass most indexers of today. Interested in Thoreau's knowledge of echoes? Simply consult the index: "Echo, an independent sound, **3**, 68; flower of sound, **4**, 14; companionability of, 492, 493. 'Echo of the Sabbath Bell heard in the Woods, The,' verse, **1**, 259. These entries are followed by several for "Echoes, **2**, 81, 82; vagaries of, **3**, 50, 51; on Hunt's farm, **4**, 492." Without an index of this sophistication and thoroughness, I could never have searched 2,730 pages of ten-point text in order to find Thoreau's thoughts on *Arum triphyllum* (contemporary name *Arisaema*) or *Genista tinctoria,* not to mention the titmouse or common crow.

Over his short life, Thoreau produced millions of words that reflected a love of solitude, a deep reverence for nature, and a respect for animals, and he even changed a few Americans' views of the world.

"It appears to me," he wrote in 1852, "that to one standing on the heights of philosophy mankind and the works of man will have sunk out of sight altogether." Man, in Thoreau's opinion, is too much insisted upon. "The poet says, 'the proper study of mankind is man.' I say, study to forget all that. Take wider views of the universe. . . . What is the village, city, state, nation, aye, the civilized world, that it should concern a man so much? The thought of them affects me, in my wisest hours, as when I pass a woodchuck's hole."

After finishing this project I realized that five people must be thanked: Ben Wechsler of Forestburgh, New York, the original woodchuck, who loves nature and fights to preserve it; the Gentlings of Asheville, for flowers, philosophy, and their garden; Sally Atwater of Stackpole Books for her advice and counsel; and my wife, Jean, for her counsel and advice.

Peter Loewer
Asheville, North Carolina
1995

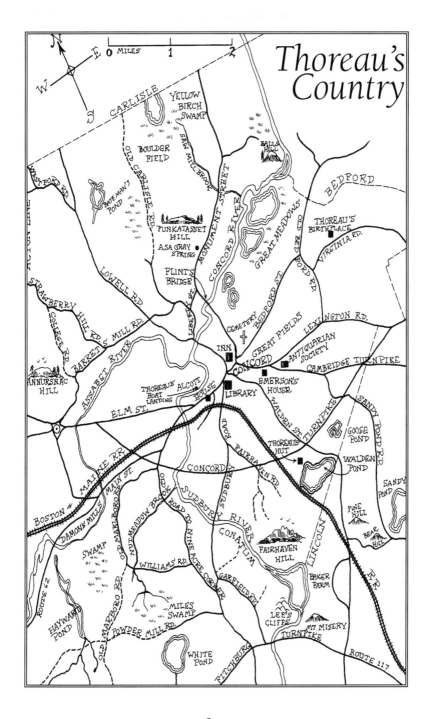

Thoreau's Country

INTRODUCTION
Henry David Thoreau

*This world and our life have practically a similar value only
to most. The value of life is what anybody will give you for
living. A man has his price at the South, is worth so many
dollars, and so he has at the North. Many a man here sets
out by saying, I will make so many dollars by such a time, or
before I die, and that is his price, as much as if he were
knocked off for it by a Southern auctioneer.*
                                        —November 29, 1860

Henry David Thoreau was born on July 12, 1817, just outside
the village of Concord, Massachusetts. Coincidentally, his birth-
day ushered in the so-called Era of Good Feelings, a phrase coined
by Boston's *Columbian Centinel,* in a salute to the new presidency of
James Monroe. Like most such salutes, it was a rash statement;
Monroe's tenure was marked by a period of great social change and
monumental disagreements about politics.

Concord, on the Concord River, was already a historic site,
having been settled in 1635. Here the Revolutionary battle of Concord was fought on April 19, 1775, now commemorated by Daniel
Chester French's bronze statue *The Minuteman.* Today many fine
old houses remain, some preserved as memorials to their noted
inhabitants, including Ralph Waldo Emerson, Nathaniel Hawthorne, the Alcott family, and Thoreau. Walden Pond is one and a
half miles south of the village, and Sleepy Hollow cemetery shel-
ters the graves of many famous Concordians. Ephraim Bull, who
developed the Concord grape within the confines of the town, is
mentioned three times in the journal. (The entry of March 24,
1856—"Mr. Bull tells me that his grapes grow faster and ripen
sooner on the west than the east side of his house"—is the only
entry concerned with grapes.)

Thoreau's mother, Cynthia, was the daughter of Asa Dunbar, a Congregational minister; his father, John Thoreau, was the son of a Protestant emigrant from the Channel Islands. At the time of his son's birth, John was an unsuccessful shopkeeper, and he, his wife, Thoreau's older sister, Helen, and his older brother, John, shared part of their house with another family. The house was said to be badly in need of paint. When Thoreau was six, his father began making graphite for pencils, a living that was never lucrative, but the family managed to get along.

In contemporary terms, Thoreau's father was the kind of man who would have been happy to sit in a Mayberry barbershop, talking with Floyd, the barber, and Andy, the sheriff, about world and local affairs. His mother was like Aunt Bee, bustling about the village, busy with community affairs, and described by an acquaintance as "next to Madam Hora, the mother of the Judge and the Senator, the most talkative person in Concord."

Thoreau's brother, John, was an amateur naturalist, an occupation that included many members of the educated classes in nineteenth-century America. Both men and women spent many free hours engaged in botanizing; armed with hand lens and sketchbook, they would take to the fields to look at plants and insects and to enjoy the day.

Thoreau attended Harvard. What remains of his writing there is largely uninspired. He did not make a mark on academe but did well enough to be listed among the commencement speakers, who numbered several dozen.

Thoreau's education did not end at Harvard, however. *Thoreau's Reading, A Study in Intellectual History with Bibliographical Catalogue,* by Robert Sattelmeyer (Princeton: Princeton University Press, 1988), documents not only the books cited in the journals but also references made in unpublished notebooks, correspondence, and the catalog of his personal library, and shows that he was an avid reader.

His interests were catholic, ranging from the classics—

Thoreau could read both Greek and Latin for pleasure, knew some French, and was acquainted with German, Italian, and Spanish— to literature to the natural sciences. He read and quoted Darwin, including *Voyage of the Beagle* and *On the Origin of Species.* He knew the works of Asa Gray, one of America's great botanists, and both *The Botanical Text Book* and *A Manual of Botany* were in his collection, not to mention John E. Sowerby's *The Ferns of Great Britain* and John George Wood's *Illustrated Natural History,* along with David Livingston's *Missionary Travels and Research in South Africa* and Baron Robert Curzon Zouche's *A Visit to the Monasteries of the Levant.*

After graduation in 1837, he began teaching in the village school, but when informed that he must whip offenders with a ferrule, a cane strengthened with a ring of metal, he resigned because corporal punishment was against his philosophy. After leaving the school, he made a trip to Maine, then began his journal entries on October 22, 1837; they continued until November 3, 1861.

Early in 1838, Henry and his brother, John, began a small school where corporal punishment was not allowed; the day began with a lecture on a moral subject, and once a week, pupils went on nature walks conducted by Henry.

In 1839 he met Ellen Sewall, a pretty woman who charmed both Henry and John. The potential for a love affair between Henry and Ellen has interested Thoreau biographers for years, but John proposed to her in the summer of 1840. A short time later she broke off the engagement, it's assumed because her parents thought the young man tainted by a much too permissive family.

> *Nature refuses to sympathize with our sorrow. She seems not to have provided for, but by a thousand contrivances against, it. She has bevelled the margins of the eyelids that the tears may not overflow on the cheek.* —*July 27, 1840*

Some scholars have hinted that Thoreau turned to nature with passion because it was a substitute for human passion. Who knows? Not everyone in this life experiences the ardor of Abelard for Heloise, the theatrics of Tristan and Isolde, or the travails of Scarlett O'Hara and Rhett Butler.

> *Nature allows of no universal secrets. The more carefully a secret is kept on one side of the globe, the larger the type it is printed in on the other. Nothing is too pointed, too personal, too immodest, for her to blazon. The relations of sex, transferred to flowers, become the study of ladies in the drawingroom. While men wear fig leaves, she grows the* Phallus impudicus *and* Phallus caninus *and other phallus-like fungi.*
> —*January 30, 1852*

In Thoreau's journals there are no graphic descriptions of the rutting of deer or the coupling of snakes. "Thoreau took it all in—" wrote Joseph Wood Krutch, "the willful woodchuck and the persistent turtle no less than the soothing woods and the bland sunset. But the red tooth and the red claw were so far from obsessing him as they were to obsess many nineteenth-century students that they play only a minor role, and even the sexuality of nature passes with no more than an occasional acknowledgment."

> Who trusted God whose love indeed,
> And love Creation's final law—
> Tho' Nature, red in tooth and claw
> With ravine, shriek'd against his creed—
> —Alfred Lord Tennyson, *In Memorium*

> *Each man's mode of speaking of the sexual relation proves how sacred his own relations of that kind are. We do not respect the mind that can jest on this subject.* —*March 4, 1852*

I know a man who never speaks of the sexual relation but jestingly, though it is a subject to be approached only with reverence and affection. What can be the character of that man's love? It is ever the subject of a stale jest, though his health or his dinner can be seriously considered. The glory of the world is seen only by a chaste mind. To whomever this fact is not an awful but beautiful mystery, there are no flowers in nature. —*July 4, 1852*

The school closed in 1841 when John Thoreau fell ill with tuberculosis and the next year died from a tetanus infection. Thoreau was devastated and went to work in his father's pencil factory.

Ralph Waldo Emerson then offered Thoreau a job as a handyman, and Thoreau accepted. For two years his payment consisted of his room and board, but he was also considered a member of Emerson's circle, through which he was introduced to the complexities of transcendentalism.

Transcendentalism was a movement that grew with exuberance, germinating in the mid-1830s and flowering until the 1860s. A New England Unitarian reaction against the conservatism of Puritanism, it turned to the philosophical principles that held sway in Europe at that time and to the teachings of the Oriental religions. American in content, the doctrine taught rugged individualism and self-reliance coupled with a belief in the existence of God in the natural world.

Practitioners included Ralph Waldo Emerson (1803–1882), respected even then as a great American poet and essayist; Frederic Henry Hedge (1805–1890), an American Unitarian clergyman and professor of ecclesiastical history at the Harvard Divinity School; George Ripley (1802–1880), an American literary critic and Unitarian minister, and one of the founders of Brook Farm (an experiment in group living at West Roxbury, Massachusetts, that flourished between 1841 and 1847 but failed because the inexperienced farmers could not profitably work the hardscrabble farm); Bronson Alcott (1799–1888), the father of Louisa May Alcott, an American educational reformer and transcendental philosopher; Margaret Fuller (1810–1850), who, though little read today, was then an influential literary critic; and Theodore Parker (1810–1860), a social reformer, leader in the fight against slavery, and advocate of prison reform.

These were the people with whom Thoreau talked long into the night—people who influenced the course of American literature for many years.

In 1842, when Nathaniel Hawthorne and his bride, Sophia Peabody—whom Hawthorne met through communications with the transcendentalists—first arrived in Concord, they asked Ralph Waldo Emerson for help in finding a gardener for their grounds. Emerson sent Thoreau, then twenty-five years old. Hawthorne described him in his journal:

". . . [of] a singular character; a young man with much of the wild original Nature still remaining in him; and so far as he is sophisticated, it is in a way and method of his own. He is as ugly as sin; long-nosed, queer-mouthed, and with uncouth and somewhat rustic manners . . . though courteous . . . corresponding with such an exterior. But his ugliness is of an honest and agreeable fashion, and becomes him much better than beauty."

Unfortunately, the only picture of Thoreau that most people have seen is the daguerreotype taken in 1856, when he began to see ill health and added a most unbecoming set of chin whiskers to what was already a formidable chin. At that time William Ellery Channing, a poet (whose works were criticized by Thoreau as being "sublimo-slipshod"), described the naturalist as having "deep set gray-blue eyes on either side of a prominent and aquiline nose (that resembled one found in all those portraits of Caesar), a full mouth with often pursed lips, and light brown, abundant hair."

On May 1, 1843, at Emerson's behest, Thoreau set off for New York City, to tutor the young son of Emerson's brother, a lawyer, who lived on Staten Island. Emerson, with only the best of motives, thought that Thoreau would benefit from the sophistication he would meet. "I walked through New York yesterday—and met no real and living person," wrote Thoreau. He remained in the city until the end of November, when he returned to Concord and moved in with his parents. About this time he found a new method of making graphite and immediately improved the financial stock of his family.

Over the years Thoreau traveled, but the following entry, about a New York visit, sums up his feelings about a big city:

> *Went to Crystal Palace; admired the houses on Fifth Avenue, the specimens of coal at the Palace, one fifty feet thick as it was cut from the mine, in the form of a square column, iron and copper ore, etc. Saw sculptures and paintings innumerable, and armor from the Tower of London, some of the Eighth Century. Saw [Horace] Greeley; Snow, the commercial editor of the* Tribune; *Solon Robinson; Fry, the musical critic, etc.; and others. Greeley carried me to the new opera house, where I heard Grisi and her troupe. First at Barnum's Museum, I saw the camelopards, said to be one eighteen the other sixteen feet high. I should say the highest stood about fifteen feet high at most. The body was only about five feet long. Why has it horns, but for ornament? Looked through his diorama, and found the houses all over the world much alike. Greeley appeared to know and be known by everybody; was admitted free to the opera, and was led by a page to various parts of the house at different times. Saw at Museum some large flakes of cutting arrowhead stone made into a sort of wide cleaves, also a hollow stone tube, probably from mounds.* —November 22, 1854

Just four days later, when he was back in the Walden woods, he penned this entry:

> *What that little long-sharp-nosed mouse I found in the Walden road to-day? Brown above, gray beneath, black incisors, five toes with claws on each foot, long snout with small blunt black extremity, many mustachios, eyes far forward, feet light or dirty white, tail 1½ inches long, whole length 3¾ inches; on causeway.*   —November 26, 1854

Thoreau was bothered by his first visit to New York City, and had troubling thoughts about Emerson and the transcendentalists. For all the powerful attractions this group of intellectuals exerted, Thoreau felt that he moved on an even higher plane. Already he was able to look at nature as it really was, a world outside the influences of religion and most philosophy. Joseph Wood Krutch writes that "even before [Thoreau] went to live in Emerson's house he had been aware of his contempt for conventional Christian moralizing, for he had noted somewhat smugly that when reading, for instance, a book on agriculture, he made it his practice to 'skip the author's moral reflections, and the words "Providence" and "He" scattered along the page, to come to the profitable level of what he has to say.' Now he wondered if much that he heard from the transcendental brothers was not the same sort of thing in different words, and if they were not contracting from their so-called nature the very disease he was trying to cure himself of."

The social life of man was beginning to push on Thoreau. Even before the trip to New York, journal entries point to a dissatisfaction with the complexities of village life.

> *I want to go soon and live away by the pond, where I shall hear only the wind whispering among the reeds. It will be success if I shall have left myself behind. But my friends ask*

what I will do when I get there. Will it not be employment
enough to watch the progress of the seasons?
                                        —December 24, 1841

The grand and solitary heart will love alone, without the
knowledge of its object. It cannot have society in its love. It
will expend its love as the cloud drops rain upon the fields
over which [it] floats. . . . I must make a part of the planet. I
must obey the law of nature.   *—March 15, 1842*

Thoreau loved Walden Pond. He had walked there most of his life. Luckily, Emerson owned some land on the edge of the pond and gave Thoreau permission to build a hut in exchange for clearing some land.

"I have thus a tight shingled and plastered house," Thoreau wrote in *Walden*, "ten feet wide by fifteen long, eight-feet posts, with a garret and a closet, a large window on each side, two trap-doors, one door at the end, and a brick fire-place opposite. The exact cost of my house, paying the usual price for such materials as I used, but not counting the work, all of which was done by myself" was exactly twenty-eight dollars, twelve and one-half cents. He moved in on July 4, 1845, an auspicious date for someone declaring independence from the social world of man.

Walden.—Yesterday I came here to live. My house makes
me think of some mountain houses I have seen, which
seemed to have a greater auroral atmosphere about them,
as I fancy of the halls of Olympus.   *—July 5, 1845*

Yet at no time was Thoreau actually cut off from the world. In January 1846, his Aunt Prudence Ward wrote a letter that mentions his living in a little house by a pond that is in view of the public road and his having many visitors, "whom he receives with pleasure."

Were they all received with pleasure? Thoreau never suffered fools gladly. In addition to friends like Emerson and Bronson Alcott, his visitors included the poet Ellery Channing, not to mention numerous hunters, trappers, folks who passed by, and even interlopers who opened his drawers and looked in his cabinets.

Eleven years later, he summed up his feelings on visitors in a journal entry:

> *I do not know how to entertain one who can't take long walks. The first thing that suggests itself is to get a horse to draw them, and that brings us at once into contact with stablers and dirty harness, and I do not get over my ride for a long time. I give up my forenoon to them and get along pretty well, the very elasticity of the air and promise of the day abetting me, but they are as heavy as dumplings by mid-afternoon. If they can't walk, why don't they take an honest nap and let me go in the afternoon? But, come two o'clock, they alarm me by an evident disposition to sit. In the midst of a most glorious Indian-summer afternoon, there they sit, breaking your chairs and wearing out the house, with their backs to the light, taking no note of the lapse of time.* —October 7, 1857

After two years at Walden, Thoreau went back to Concord. He continued to write in his journals, lectured occasionally, and did various odd jobs around Concord, including gardening, painting, fence building, and carpentry. He also began his work as a surveyor for the town.

> *I can easily walk ten, fifteen, twenty, any number of miles, commencing at my own door, without going by any house, without crossing a road except where the fox and the mink do. Concord is the oldest inland town in New England, perhaps in the States, and the walker is peculiarly favored here.*

There are square miles in my vicinity which have no in-habitant. First along by the river, and then the brook, and then the meadow and the woodside. Such solitude! From a hundred hills I can see civilization and abodes of man afar. These farmers and their works are scarcely more obvious than woodchucks.   —*July 1850*

I am sure that my acquaintances mistake me. I am not the man they take me for. On a little nearer view they would find me out. They ask my advice on high matters, but they do not even know how poorly on't I am for hats and shoes. I have hardly a shift. Just as shabby as I am in my outward apparel,—aye, and more lamentably shabby, for nakedness is not so bad a condition after all,—am I in my inward apparel. If I should turn myself inside out, my rags and meanness would appear. I am something to him that made me, undoubtedly, but not much to any other that he has made. All I can say is that I live and breathe and have my thoughts.   —*July 1850*

During May 1861, Thoreau traveled west in search of the health that he felt was fading. He came back in worse shape than when he left. Journal entries continue until November 3, 1861. That day he wrote about a hornets' nest in a nearby maple tree; about four newly born kittens; and about Edward Lord Herbert's autobiographical remarks on shirts, waistcoats, other garments, and the staleness of his breath due to tobacco.

Later in the day he recorded the progress of one kitten: "You would say that this little creature was as perfectly protected by its instinct in its infancy as an old man can be by his wisdom."

That night, he made the final entry:

After a violent easterly storm in the night . . . I notice that the surface of the railroad causeway, composed of gravel, is

singularly marked . . . so that I can tell within a small frac-
tion of a degree from what quarter the rain came. These
lines . . . are perfectly parallel, and straight as a ruler, diag-
onally across the flat surface of the causeway for its whole
length. [T]he heavy drops driven almost horizontally have
washed out a furrow on each side, and on all sides are these
ridges, half an inch apart and perfectly parallel.

All this is perfectly distinct to an observant eye, and yet
could easily pass unnoticed by most. Thus each wind is self-
registering.

He was now hardly able to sleep, and his days of walking the
woods were over.

On April 6, 1862, President Lincoln demanded the immediate
surrender of Fort Sumter. On April 15, Lincoln called for 75,000
volunteers to put down the insurrection. The Civil War began.

Thoreau hated the institution of slavery, he hated war, he dis-
trusted politicians, and he knew that society was, in the words of
Krutch, "out of joint." He died on the morning of May 6, 1862.

Books have been written about Thoreau's effect on America's
psyche, but it's interesting to note that even today his name is used
(often in vain) to market nature to a starved populace. Recently, an
Arizona resort advertised its extravagant health spa, pool, and
restaurant by telling potential visitors that Thoreau would never
have settled for a log cabin if he had known about their twenty
acres of Spanish-style architecture and world-class facilities!

Walden is what he's remembered for but the journal is, to me,
the most precious thing he left.

And then for my afternoon walks I have a garden, larger
than any artificial garden that I have read of and far more
attractive to me,—mile after mile of embowered walks,
such as no nobleman's ground can boast, with animals run-
ning free and wild therein as from the first,—varied with

land and water prospect, and, above all, so retired that it is
extremely rare that I meet a single wanderer in its mazes.
No gardener is seen therein, not gates nor [sic]. You may
wander away to solitary bowers and brooks and hills.
                                                    —June 20, 1850

Most of us lack the opportunities to wander the land that
Thoreau wandered. *Thoreau's Garden* thrives in the imagination.
Here we can enjoy the plants that he wrote about in the journal—
plants that I also have affection for—and learn their history, their
uses, and their charms. Perhaps in a world where oceans are rising,
summers are hotter, winters colder, and a beneficent sun has become a bit crueler, the best garden is a garden of the mind.

To live to a good old age such as the ancients reached, serene
and contented, dignifying the life of man, leading a simple,
epic country life in those days of confusion and turmoil . . .
retaining the tastes and the innocence of his youth, There is
. . . nothing so cheering and world-famous as this.
                                                    —Undated 1854

ON SCIENTIFIC NAMES

I have no objection to giving the names of some naturalists,
men of flowers, to plants, if by their lives they have identified
themselves with them. There may be a few Kalmias. But it must
be done very sparingly, or, rather, discriminatingly, and no
man's name be used who has not been such a lover of flowers
that the flowers themselves may be supposed thus to recipro-
cate his love.   —*August 31, 1851*

Thoreau realized that some common names for plants have
originated in a mere blunder. The *Citharexylum melanocardium*
[fruticosum] of the West Indies is known to the French as *fidèle*,
from its faithfulness or durability in building, a name the English
corrupted into fiddlewood; the wood, however, is unfit for musical
instruments.

Thoreau saluted the common man's names: "How good a
name!" he exclaimed of the wayfarer's tree. "Who bestowed it?
How did it get adopted? The mass of men are very unpoetic, yet
that Adam that names things is a poet. The boor is ready to accept
the name the poet gives. How nameless is the poet among us! He is
abroad, but is not recognized. He does not get crowned with the
laurel."

But the botanical life isn't always easy. Thoreau expressed frus-
tration about a particular rush that for twenty years had kept him
from describing some of its peculiarities because he didn't know
its name or anybody in the neighborhood who did. "After all," he
mused, "with the knowledge of the name comes a distincter recog-
nition and knowledge of the thing. . . . My knowledge now becomes communicable and grows by communication. I can now
learn what others know about the same thing."

Scientific names as applied to botanical subjects are fascinating, especially because they meld the words of the past with those
of the present in combinations that delight neologists and most
etymologists. But when it comes to common names, even the
hardiest wordsmiths are sometimes at a loss.

Many times scientific names are easier to understand than common names because they often combine well-documented Greek or Latin words that apply in some way to the plants they name. But even then problems of interpretation arise: nobody knows where the name *Cleome* came from, other than that Theophrastus used it in 300 B.C., or *Lonas,* the genus of a charming little yellow annual with a name beyond anyone's ken. However, in the case of the *Arctium lappa,* the great burdock, *Arctium* is from the Greek word *arktos,* for bear, referring to the plant's many coarse bristles, and *lappa* is Latin for bur, names that apply nicely to the plant.

There is a move on in publishing—especially popular magazines—to "glitz it up and dumb it down." Many editors and publishers now believe that the public cannot deal with Latin names for plants. Using only popular names is fine as long as you are dealing with dahlias and delphiniums (those two common names, by the way, are also those plants' Latin names). But as soon as you branch out into unusual annuals and perennials, you will find that common names change not only from country to country but even from region to region.

Take, for example, just the English names for the great burdock described above, a plant originally from Europe and now naturalized over most of North America. In his book *The Englishman's Flora,* Geoffrey Grigson lists fifty-two common names for this plant. A few of the choicer appellations are bachelor's buttons (since bachelors can't sew and would use the Velcro approach to buttoning up), butter-dock (since the large leaves were used to wrap butter), clog-weed (self-explanatory), snake's rhubarb (a sly dig at the people who eat the young shoots either cooked or raw), tuzzy-muzzy (referring to the original usage of being disheveled and ragged), and cuckholdy-burr-busses (I'll leave that one alone).

Now imagine what will happen over the years as the spirit of education commingles with the god of the mall, and people not only talk less but read less and books all succumb to the ravages of acidic paper: in another hundred years who will know what these names mean?

All known plants are given Latin, or scientific, names, and each name is unique. And they are easily understood throughout the world. Whether in Japan, Saudi Arabia, Russia, or Chicago, and regardless of the language spoken by the native gardener, *Cynara scolymus* is the artichoke and *Taraxacum officinale* is the common dandelion.

Four terms are in general use: *genus, species, variety,* and *cultivar.* In print, the genus and species are set off from the accompanying text by the use of italic type, and if the text is italic, the scientific name is set in roman type. The *genus* name refers to a group of plants that are closely related; the *species* name suggests an individual plant's unique quality or color, or perhaps honors the individual who discovered it. Usually, the genus has an initial capital letter and the species a lowercase one, but when the species is derived from a former generic name, a person's name, or a common name, it too can begin with a capital letter.

The variety is also italicized and usually preceded by the abbreviation "var." in roman type. A *variety* is a plant that develops a noticeable change that breeds true from generation to generation. A *cultivar* is a variation that appears in a plant while in cultivation (thus a change by either chance or design). The word is derived from "*culti*vated *var*iety," and the names of cultivars are distinguished by roman type inside single quotation marks.

Thus the common biennial garden flower called the foxglove has the scientific name *Digitalis purpurea.* The genus name is Latin for the finger of a glove and refers to the shape of the blossom, and the species name refers to the usual color of the flower. Biennial means it lives for two growing seasons, compared with the one season of an annual and the many seasons of a perennial. There is a cultivar called 'Foxy' that blooms the first year. And though it seems to violate a well-known rule of copyediting, any punctuation marks used after the single quotation mark of a cultivar name follow that mark and do not fall within it.

THE SERVICEBERRY
Amelanchier spp.

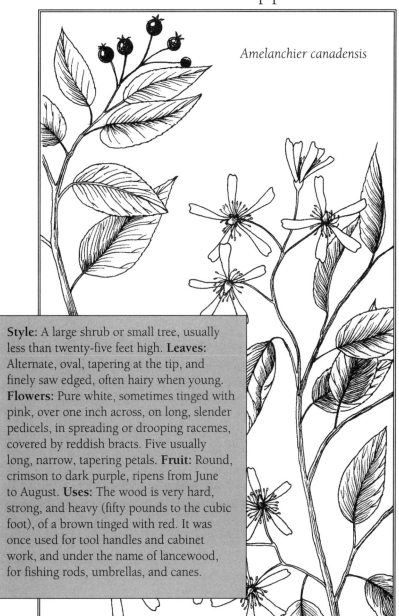

Amelanchier canadensis

Style: A large shrub or small tree, usually less than twenty-five feet high. **Leaves:** Alternate, oval, tapering at the tip, and finely saw edged, often hairy when young. **Flowers:** Pure white, sometimes tinged with pink, over one inch across, on long, slender pedicels, in spreading or drooping racemes, covered by reddish bracts. Five usually long, narrow, tapering petals. **Fruit:** Round, crimson to dark purple, ripens from June to August. **Uses:** The wood is very hard, strong, and heavy (fifty pounds to the cubic foot), of a brown tinged with red. It was once used for tool handles and cabinet work, and under the name of lancewood, for fishing rods, umbrellas, and canes.

The shad-bush in blossom is the first to show like a fruit tree,—like a pale peach,—on the hillsides, seen afar amid gray twigs, amid leafless shrub oaks, etc., before even its own leaves are much expanded.   —*May 10, 1854*

I see where the farmer mending his fence has just cut one to make part of the fence, and it is stretched out horizontally, a mass of white bloom.   —*May 10, 1858*

U p in Walden, depending on the New England winter, the serviceberry, or shadbush, begins to bloom in early to mid-May. The spring blooms of this tree always gladden a heart still weighted down with the memory of endless snow and ice.

Even in midwinter, when the sky is a darker shade than the bark of the tree, a serviceberry is a beautiful sight, especially when the many bare branches are viewed through a cloud of snowflakes. But coming upon that blooming tree in spring is like approaching a burst of galaxies at universe center: shining white lights surrounded by nothing.

In 1853, Thoreau wrote that farmers of the day said things like "Well, though I have lived seventy years, I never saw nor heard of them." Most woodswalkers and hunters probably preferred warmer weather for stalking birds and late fall for tracking deer, and were rarely walking the hedgerows or forest roads when the shadbush was in bloom.

In many parts of the country, the blooming time of shadbush is too early for wild or domestic honeybees, so the flowers are generally pollinated by little dark brown or black female bees of the Andrena tribe. They live in burrows rather than hives, some digging numerous branched tunnels and some content to dwell in a simple straight tunnel.

Many Americans call it the shadbush because in the Northeast, about the time the first blossoms opened, the inland waters flowed free after a winter's freezing, and American shad (*Alosa sapidissima)* would run up the streams and rivers. But that's only one of the many common names for this tree, which include Juneberry, serviceberry, sarviceberry, Maycherry, Saskatoon, shadblow, Indian pear, sugar pear, sweet pear, grape pear, sugar plum currant tree, and Western serviceberry.

In his book *Growing & Propagating Showy Native Woody Plants* (Chapel Hill: University of North Carolina Press, 1992), Dick Bir notes of hearing the origin of the name "service" or "sarvice." He writes that because of the ground freezing solid, anyone who died in the winter had to wait for the thawing of the earth for burial, which often occurred when the shadbush bloomed.

Another interpretation is that the tree that bears also serves, hence service tree and serviceberry. Were it that simple. In actuality, the name of this plant has English roots. The amelanchiers of America and the service trees of England both bloom in May and both have usable fruit. The American trees were thought to be close relatives of the wild service tree, *Sorbus torminalis,* and the service tree, *S. domestica.* Introduced to England from Europe and North Africa, *S. torminalis* bears fruit described as being best used to settle the stomach, for colic, or for "green sickness" in virgins, a malady I've not been able to pinpoint. *S. domestica* was also introduced to England; John Tradescant brought it from the Mediterranean region. The bark was formerly used for tanning leather, and after being touched with frost, the fruits are still used as food. So "service" came from "serves," from the Old English word *syrfe,* which is from the Latin *sorbus.* The derivation of the scientific name is far simpler, coming from the Provençal French name of the European species, *Amelanchier ovalis.*

Another use of the service tree clan should be mentioned. *The Oxford English Dictionary* notes that in Scotland in the late 1700s, service tree branches were fixed above the stakes of tied cattle to ward off elves and witches.

Gathering the fruits of the serviceberry is far easier described than done. The round, dark red to purple pomes (the correct name for the fruits of members of the rose family) have a sweet and pleasant odor and taste that is attractive to both people and birds—not to mention chipmunks, squirrels, deer, and mountain goats—and unless you net the trees, the animals usually get there first. The pomes usually ripen in June, but at higher elevations (above 2,500 feet) it's mid-July, or farther north, even August.

If you're lucky with your netting, you can make a superior jelly and jam from the fruits, not to mention great pies and sauces. Unlike many wild foods, serviceberries are very good to eat and do not taste like pasteboard with seeds.

I have an undated copy of a booklet entitled *Food Plants of the North American Indians* (Misc. Publication 237, U.S. Department of Agriculture) that says the fruit of the service trees and bushes were used both fresh and dried; the pomes were boiled and eaten with meat or added to pemmican (sun-dried, thin slices of pounded buffalo or venison, packed with animal fat), and a tea was made from the dried leaves. Sometimes the material was dried for winter use. The Chippewas used a root bark tea of serviceberry mixed with other herbs as a tonic for excessive menstrual bleeding and digestive disturbances.

I find apparently two varieties of the amelanchier,—the first I noticed, with smooth reddish delicate leaves and somewhat linear petals and loose racemes, petals sometimes pinkish; the second to-day, perhaps a little later than the first, leaves light-colored and downy and petals broader and perhaps not quite so long as the first, racemes more crowded. I am not sure that this is the variety oblongifolia *of Gray. [A footnote to the 1906 edition of the journal states that this tree might be* Pyrus ovalis, *or the swamp pyrus.] —May 4, 1853*

Saw an amelanchier with downy leaf (apparently oblongifolia) *on the southeast edge of Yellow Birch Swamp, about*

*eighteen feet high and five or six inches in diameter,—a
clump of them about as big as an apple tree. —May 13, 1855*

It's likely that the trees Thoreau saw were *Amelanchier lamarckii*,
with white flowers, tinged with pink, which reaches a height of
thirty feet; *A. arborea*, which is usually a tall shrub but can reach a
height of thirty-three feet; and *A. laevis*, a species that can attain
fifty feet and is responsible for the cultivar 'Rosea', with lovely pink
flowers, and 'Prince William', a form with multiple stems and blue
fruits.

Unfortunately, the nomenclature of serviceberries has not got-
ten any better over the years, and today, to cut down on confusion,
many nurseries have created their own species. Catalogs now often
speak of *Amelanchier grandiflora*, or from the more careful nursery-
folk, *Amelanchier* x *grandiflora*, signifying that the new varieties
are hybrids. Among the most popular today are 'Robin Hill', with
pink flower buds and yellow-red fall color, and 'Cole's Select', with
white flowers and red foliage in fall; these hybrids are hardy
through Zone 5.

In addition to the common serviceberry *(Amelanchier canadensis)*, the Allegheny serviceberry *(A. laevis)*, good for Zones 4
through 8, has lovely white flowers and foliage that has a purple
cast when young.

The Saskatoon serviceberry *(Amelanchier alnifolia)* is a smaller
species, staying about fifteen feet high, that tolerates a soil pH of
5.0 to 6.0 and is hardy through Zone 6.

THE BOG ROSEMARY
Andromeda polifolia

Style: A small, straggly shrub, usually under a foot high, with lovely flowers. **Leaves:** Thin and oblong between five-eighths and an inch and a half long, with a white bloom on the undersides and curled margins. **Flowers:** Pale pink to near white in nodding umbels. **Fruit:** A pear-shaped capsule. **Uses:** Rock gardens, wild gardens, and neat borders. **Culture:** Needs well-drained but moist, acid soil, with plenty of humus; except for the far north, needs some shade; very cold hardy.

Saw something blue, or glaucous, at Beck Stow's Swamp today; approached and discovered the Andromeda polifolia, *in the midst of the swamp at the north end, not long since out of bloom. This is another instance of a common experience. When I am shown from abroad, or hear of, or in any [way] become interested in, some plant or other thing, I am pretty sure to find it soon. Within a week R. W. E. showed me a slip of this in a botany, as a great rarity which George Bradford brought from Watertown. I had long been interested in it by Linnaeus's account. I now find it in abundance. It is a neat and tender-looking plant, with the pearly new shoots now half a dozen inches long and the singular narrow revolute leaves. I suspect the flower adds much to it.*

—July 14, 1853

The bog rosemary also bears the common names of wild rosemary, water andromeda, March Holy Rose, and moorwort.

Linnaeus was so enamored of this subshrub that he likened the pink of its flowers to "a fine female complexion." He named the genus after Andromeda, the daughter of King Cepheus, who was delivered from a prodigious sea dragon by Perseus, as she stood bound to a rock surrounded by a tormented sea. Linnaeus wrote, "This plant is always fixed on some little turfy hillock in the midst of the swamps, just as Andromeda herself was chained to a rock in the sea, which bathed her feet as the fresh water does the roots of this plant."

In February 1854, the foliage of the bog rosemary still struck Thoreau's fancy.

The handsome lanceolate leaves of the Andromeda polifolia, *dark but pure and uniform dull red above, strongly revolute, and of a delicate bluish white beneath, deserve to be copied onto works of art. Many [leaves] in which the con-*

*trast [between upper and lower surfaces] is finest are
narrow, revolute leaves, like the delicate and beautiful
Andromeda polifolia, the ledum [Ledum spp.], Kalmia
glauca."*   —*February 18, 1854*

At this point in the narrative Thoreau stops to ruminate about
De Quincey's remark that "'the ancients had no experimental
knowledge of severe climates.' Neither have the English at home
compared with us of New England, nor we, compared with the
Esquimaux."

Although garden authorities like Norman Taylor have called
the plant confined to northern bogs and unsuited to warm regions,
the adaptable bog rosemary will do very well into USDA Zone 8 as
long as it gets summer shade and ample moisture. There are a
number of available cultivars: 'Kiri-Kaming' is a dwarf Japanese
form that reaches eight inches and bears dark, red-tinged leaves;
'Macrophylla' has broad, dark green leaves with very large deep
pink flowers; 'Nana', the typical dwarf form, grows to eight inches;
and 'Nana Alba' has pure white flowers against a showy, silver blue
foliage. *Hortus Third* lists a cultivar called 'Montana', a compact
plant with dark leaves.

While looking for the lovely bog rosemary, Thoreau continued
to be aware of the life around it.

In woods by Andromeda polifolia *the chestnut-sided war-
bler, with clear yellow crown and yellow on wings and chestnut sides. It is exploring low trees and bushes, often along
stems about young leaves, and frequently or after short
pauses utters its somewhat summer-yellowbird-like note,
say,* tchip, tchip, chip chip *(quick),* tche tche ter tchéa,
—*spray[ey] and rasping and faint. Another, further off. . . .*
Andromeda polifolia *now in prime, but the leaves are apt
to be blackened and unsightly, and the flowers, though deli-*

cate, have a feeble and sickly look, rose-white, somewhat
crystalline. Its new shoots or new leaves, unfolding, say
when it flowered or directly after, now one inch long.

—*May 24, 1855*

Earlier that year on a morning in January, as Thoreau was walking though Holden's white spruce swamp, he spotted two other beautiful bog plants. The first was *Andromeda calyculata,* with delicate evergreen shoots very much like *polifolia,* peeping above the crust of the snow; the second was *Kalmia glauca* var. *rosmarinifolia,* with delicate evergreen leaves growing in an opposite manner, each strongly revolute, somewhat reddish green above. Upon further investigation, Thoreau described the leaves as slightly weather-beaten ("imbrowned or ripened by the winter, as it were" and "its cheeks made ruddy by the cold") and white glaucous beneath with a yellow midrib (not veined, mucronated, or alternated like *A. polifolia*), growing on the ends of the twigs, which were sharply two edged. The flower buds were quite conspicuous, arranged crosswise in the axils of the leaves as he looked down on them. The entire plant appeared more tender and yellowish than bog rosemary.

Thoreau's *Andromeda calyculata* turns out to be the leather-leaf or dwarf Cassandra, genus *Chamaedaphne.* There's only one species in this genus, and that is a low, evergreen shrub that also grows in bogs. Hardy to USDA Zone 2, it's described in *Hortus Third* as a good shrub for the rock garden, reaching a height of about four feet; the cultivar 'Nana' grows only about a foot high. The nodding white flowers that grow in a one-sided raceme resemble little bells, and thanks to the chill of its native haunts, it often begins to bloom before the snows have gone.

Here's where *Andromeda* nomenclature gets a bit involved. After Thoreau's time, this lovely plant was moved to the genus *Cassandra,* but like its namesake (the Trojan prophetess who foretold the coming of the Greeks but was ignored), *Cassandra* was abandoned and the plant moved to the genus *Chamaedaphne,* becoming *Chamaedaphne calyculata* but keeping the common name of Cassandra. *Chamaedaphne* is a blend of two Greek words, *chamae,* which means "low to the ground," and *Daphne,* the maiden who scorned Apollo's love and was changed into a laurel tree.

Kalmia glauca var. *rosmarinifolia* had its species name changed to *polifolia,* but everything else stayed the same, its common names being the rosemary-leafed laurel and the alpine bog laurel.

> *A cloudy day, threatening snow; wet under foot. . . . I am attracted at this season by the fine bright-red buds of the privet andromeda, sleeping couchant along the slender light-brown twigs. They look brightest against a dark ground. I notice the pink shoots of low blueberries where they are thick.* —January 9, 1855

In Holden's swamp, so remote in the mid-1800s, in addition to *Andromeda polifolia* and *Kalmia glauca,* Thoreau found the dwarf huckleberry, or *Gaylussacia dumosa,* and the small-leaf bog cranberry, or *Vaccinium oxycoccus,* plants that, according to Thoreau, scarcely a citizen of Concord ever saw. "It would be as novel to them to stand there as in a conservatory, or in Greenland," he notes. The dwarf huckleberry and the dwarf cranberry are two more beauties for the rock or wild garden.

I've yet to find a source for *Gaylussacia dumosa,* or the dwarf huckleberry (named for J. L. Gay-Lussac, a celebrated French chemist), a deciduous shrub with white to pink bell-like blossoms followed by round black berries.

The dwarf huckleberry was described by Thoreau as usually an inconspicuous bush, eight to twelve inches high, bending over the sphagnum in which it grows. He was impressed by the flower, especially the very large and peculiar bell-shaped corolla, adorned with prominent ribs and having a rosy tinge. It is not to be mistaken for the edible huckleberry (*Vaccinium* spp.). Vaccinium is said to be an old Latin name of disputed origin, used by Virgil and Pliny and probably a corruption of the word *Hyacinthus.*

> *As for the* Vaccinia, *I am disposed to agree with those who derive the name from* bacca, *a berry, for one species or another of this large family is the berry of berries in most northern parts of the world. They form an under-shrub, or sort of lower forest, even throughout our woodlands generally, to say nothing of open fields and hills. They form a humble and more or less dormant, but yet vivacious forest under a forest, which bides its time.*   —*November 2, 1860*

The box huckleberry (*Gaylussacia brachycera*) is a native treasure overlooked by Thoreau. The plant has glossy evergreen leaves that take on a reddish tinge in the wintertime; the lovely, pink-tinged blue flowers are followed by dark blue berries. This shrub reaches a height of only five to six inches and will slowly spread out two feet wide.

The small-leaf bog cranberry (*Vaccinium oxycoccus*) sprouts tiny leaves on wiry stems that creep along the ground. It bears pink flowers followed by edible red cranberries, but don't stand in line, because it would take quite a number of mature plants to produce enough for even a cup of jam, not to mention enough to grace a goose.

> *I look for* Vaccinium oxycoccus *in the swamp. The uneven surface of the sphagnum in which the slender vine grows comes up to my idea of a mountainous country better than many actual mountains that I have seen. Labrador mountains these are at least. The higher patches of sphagnum are changed to a dark purple, which shows a crude green where you crack it by your weight. The lower parts are yet yellowish-green merely. These interesting little cranberries are quite scarce, the vine bearing (this year, at least) only amid*

the higher and drier sphagnous mountains amid the lowest bushes about the edge of the open swamp. There the dark-red berries (quite ripe) now rest, on the shelves and in the recesses of the red sphagnum. There is only enough of these berries for sauce to a botanist's Thanksgiving dinner.

—October 16, 1859

THE BEARBERRY
Arctostaphylos uva-ursi

Style: A prostrate and spreading shrub never more than a foot high. Branches are usually twelve to twenty-four inches long, rooting at the joints, but over a long period of time can reach many feet. **Leaves:** Leathery evergreen leaves are spatulate and about an inch long; they turn bronze in the winter. **Flowers:** Little urn-shaped flowers are pink or white. **Fruit:** The fruit is red. **Zone:** 2. **Uses:** Great for the rock garden, especially when the plants can trail over the edge of a rock wall. **Culture:** Bearberries do best in a light sandy soil or a scree mix of small gravel and soil. Provide full sun or partial shade.

When we go ashore and ramble inland below Carlisle Bridge, find here and there the freshly cut woodpiles which the choppers haven't yet carted off, the ground strewn with chips. A field lately cleared (last fall perhaps), with charred stumps, and grain now greening the sandy and uneven soil, reminds me agreeably of a new country. Found a large bed of Arbutus uva-ursi with fruit in Carlisle half a mile below bridge. Some of the berries were turned black, as well as the berried stems and leaves next to the ground at bottom of the thick beds—an inky black. This vine red in the sunniest places. Never saw its fruit in this neighborhood before.

—April 10, 1852

In Thoreau's time, the bearberry had the genus name *Arbutus* because of its resemblance to the trailing arbutus.

The modern scientific name breaks down to the Greek words *arktos,* for bear, and *staphyle,* for berry. The species name *uva* is Latin for a pulpy fruit like a grape, and *ursi* is Latin for bear. So the name really means "bear-berry-grape-bear," all referring to the long history of bears supposedly eating the fruit. In fact, Thoreau's first mention of bearberry occurred on July 14, 1858, when he recorded a quote about *Arctostaphylos uva-ursi* from the *Encyclopedia of Agriculture* by John Loudon: "In Sweden, Russia, and America they [the berries] form a principal part of the food of bears."

In addition to the most common name of bearberry, this wonderful little shrub is called kinnikinnick, red bearberry, hog cranberry, sandberry, mountain box, bear's grape, and mealberry. Other less common names include universe-vine, crow-berry, barren myrtle, and bilberry. Local names from England and Scotland include the marvelous rapper-dandy, Burren myrtle (from growing on Burren limestone), gnashicks, creashak, blanchnog, and moanagus.

Kinnikinnick is an American Indian word that literally means a mixture; it refers to a mix of dried leaves and the bark of certain plants used by the Indians for smoking either alone or with added tobacco. Among the chosen species were the red bearberry, the silky cornel (*Cornus amomum*), and sometimes the red-osier dogwood (*C. stolonifera*). As to the name rapper-dandy, I can think of only one origin: in old English (even in new English), the word rapper can mean a lie or outrageous statement—and the red berry certainly looks a lot better than it tastes. Its mealy texture—soft, dry, and none too good—accounts for the name mealberry. As to the other odd names from England, I haven't a clue, although blanchnog might refer to cooking the berries in nog, an old name for an English beer. Bearberry is called *Raisin d'ours* and *Busserole* in France and *Bärentraube* in Germany.

There are about fifty species in the genus, all called bearberries or sometimes manzanita, the second name coming from the California plant *Arctostaphylos manzanita*. Bearberries are found in dry, sandy, or rocky soil from Labrador across the Arctic to Alaska, and south to a line stretching from New Jersey across the country to California, not to mention Northern Europe and Asia. Way up in the Canadian Arctic there are two other plants for scree conditions: *A. alpina,* the Alpine bearberry, is a trailing shrub with shreddy bark and long-lasting leaves that turn a deep red in the fall; its fruit is black and insipid. *A. rubra* is a similar plant but its leaves are deciduous, and the fruit, although scarlet and very juicy, is also insipid. Insipid, by the way, is from *sapidus,* the Latin word for savory; *insipid* means lacking taste.

> *The bear-berry* (Arbutus uva-ursi) *in bloom, a neat bell-like flower with a red contracted rim, clear pearly and red, a reddish tinge and red lips, transparent at base.*
> —*May 14, 1852*

Bumblebees are the bearberry's chief pollinators, and the resulting berries are eaten by a number of birds that are probably the main distributors of these plants from Labrador to Alaska.

There are other values to bearberry. Its large mats of growth—eventually fifteen feet across or more—manufacture valuable humus that eventually allows other plants to grow. In Sweden the leaves are used to tan leather. From a medical perspective, the dried leaves are used for a tea that is strongly diuretic and very astringent. It's valuable as a urinary tract antiseptic for cystitis and for relieving diarrhea, and was once used to treat kidney and gall stones, bronchitis, and gonorrhea, and to stop bleeding. But there are contraindications to its use because of the presence of arbutin, a chemical that can be toxic to kidney function.

Although the berries are edible raw, old books always advise that the taste improves with cooking, especially when other berries, like blueberries, are added to the mix.

Amazingly enough, for such a slow-growing and, at least from the commercial point of view, unimportant plant, there are a number of cultivars. 'Alaska' is prostrate and has round, dark green leaves that are smaller than the species; 'Big Bear' has large leaves of a shiny dark green and large red berries; 'Convict Lake' is a very small-growing form; 'Emerald Carpet' has leaves of a very deep green in contrast to pink flowers; 'Massachusetts' is tolerant of wet conditions and is of medium size; 'Pt. Reyes' is more vigorous than the species, with dark green leaves and mahogany-colored berries; 'Radiant' produces a heavy crop of large, bright red fruits; 'Thymifolia' is an arctic form with very small leaves; 'Vancouver Jade' has lush, jade green foliage surrounding pink flowers; 'Wood's Red' is a dwarf form with small, dark green leaves and fine reddish color in winter; and 'Microphylla' is a form with very small leaves.

In closing, I can't resist a personal footnote about bearberry. I once served two years in the U.S. Army and received my basic training at Fort Dix, New Jersey. One fine afternoon in early autumn, our platoon was out on maneuvers at the edge of the Pine Barrens, a stretch of land that has an incredible selection of wild plants. We were dressed in fatigues and carried heavy packs on our backs, and the still-bright sun was turning the air uncomfortably warm. Without warning two planes swooped over our heads to "bomb" us with bags of flour.

"Everybody off the road," our sergeant yelled. "Hit the deck at the edge of the woods!"

Most of us were spared being dusted with Pillsbury's Best. I found myself near a small pile of rocks, a collection of fine mosses, and a big clump of bearberry full of red fruit. I was enchanted by the plant and my eyes lingered on its every feature. So intent was my examination that I was not aware of our sergeant until he began to kick me on the bottom of my boots.

"Just what do you think you're doing there, Loewer?"

I hesitated to confess my interest in wild plants because, frankly, he wasn't that type of guy.

"Just felt a bit faint," I said. "It must be the heat."

> *That most men can be easily transplanted from here to there, for [bearberries] have so little root,—no tap root,— or their roots penetrate so little way, that you can thrust a shovel quite under them and take them up, roots and all.*
> —*May 14, 1852*

I, for one, was not easily transplanted to Fort Dix.

THE SWAMP PINK
Arethusa bulbosa

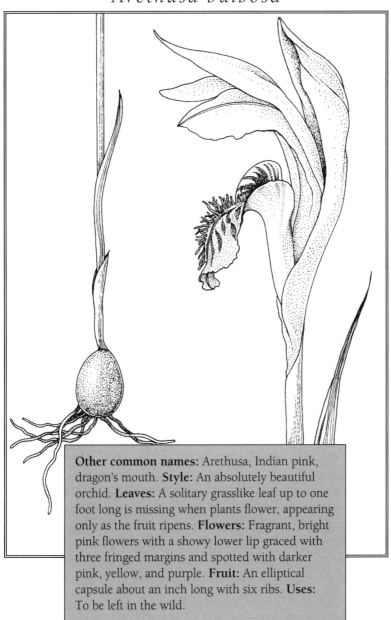

Other common names: Arethusa, Indian pink, dragon's mouth. **Style:** An absolutely beautiful orchid. **Leaves:** A solitary grasslike leaf up to one foot long is missing when plants flower, appearing only as the fruit ripens. **Flowers:** Fragrant, bright pink flowers with a showy lower lip graced with three fringed margins and spotted with darker pink, yellow, and purple. **Fruit:** An elliptical capsule about an inch long with six ribs. **Uses:** To be left in the wild.

The bulbous arethusa, the most splendid, rich, and high-colored flower thus far, methinks, all flower and color, almost without leaves, and looking much larger than it is, and more conspicuous on account of its intense color. A flower of mark. It appeared two or three times as large as reality when it flashed upon me from the meadow. Bigelow [Jacob Bigelow, author of American Medical Botany*] calls it a "crystalline purple,"* . . . *[and] some poet must sing in praise of the bulbous arethusa.* —June 3, 1852

The Greek goddess Diana changed the woodland nymph Arethusa into a fountain to save her from the amorous river god Alpheus, who pursued the young beauty after she refreshed herself in a shaded stream. It's a fitting name for this most glamorous of orchids—also known as the Indian pink or the dragon's mouth—not only because of its beauty but also because it revels in the moist surroundings of sphagnum bogs, shallow swamps, and wet meadows.

There are two species of this orchid, one American and one Japanese (*Arethusa japonica*), and it's rare in both countries. Since living in North Carolina, I've seen the flower only twice, on both occasions in acid sphagnum bogs.

Thoreau saw the flowers again at the end of May in 1853, and was still impressed by their beauty. He also noted that the damselflies were beginning to stir about that time.

Already the ringing croak of a toad begins to be heard here and there along the river, and the troonk of a bullfrog from time to time. . . . *Our river has so little current that when the wind has gone down, as at present, it is dark and perfectly smooth, and at present dusty as a stagnant pool in every part of it; far from there being any murmur, there is no ripple nor eddy for the most part.* . . . *The bulbous arethusa out a day or two—probably yesterday. Though in a measure prepared for it, still its beauty surprised me; it is by far the highest and richest color yet. Its intense color in the midst of the green meadow made it look twice as large as reality; it looks very foreign in the midst of our plants—its richly speckled, curled, and bearded lip. Devil's-needles begin to fly; saw one the 14th.*   *—May 28, 1853*

According to Neltje Blanchan in *Nature's Garden* (New York: Doubleday, Page & Company, 1904), each cormlike bulb produces a single flower that rarely develops seed. "[It's] a temptingly beautiful prize," she wrote, "which few may refrain from carrying home, to have it wither on the way . . . little wonder this exquisite orchid is rare and that from certain of those cranberry bogs of Eastern New England, which it formerly brightened with its vivid pink, it has now gone forever."

Thoreau was surprised to find these orchids abundant in Hubbard's Close, a swampy area between Walden Road and the Cambridge Turnpike.

It is so leafless that it shoots up unexpectedly. It is all color, a little hook of purple flame projecting from the meadow into the air. Some are comparatively pale. This high-colored plant shoots up suddenly, all flower, in meadows where it is wet walking. A superb flower.   *—June 9, 1854*

A week later Thoreau noted that the fragrance of the arethusa was like that of the lady's-slipper.

Miss Blanchan notes that this orchid is beloved by the bumblebee, an insect that seems to know that moisture-loving plants secrete the most nectar. The flower's unusual liplike petal acts as a landing pad for the insect, encouraging it to enter the flower in search of sugary food. As the bee leaves, the lid of the helmet-shaped anther drops a few soft pellets of pollen on the black fur of its head. When the bee visits the next arethusa, that head, now decked with golden pollen, rubs against the long, sticky stigma of the new flower and ensures the cross pollination of these beautiful blossoms.

Only in Thoreau's Garden does the arethusa still bloom in profusion every spring. In the real world, each year sees less and less of its beauty.

THE JACK-IN-THE-PULPIT
Arisaema triphyllum

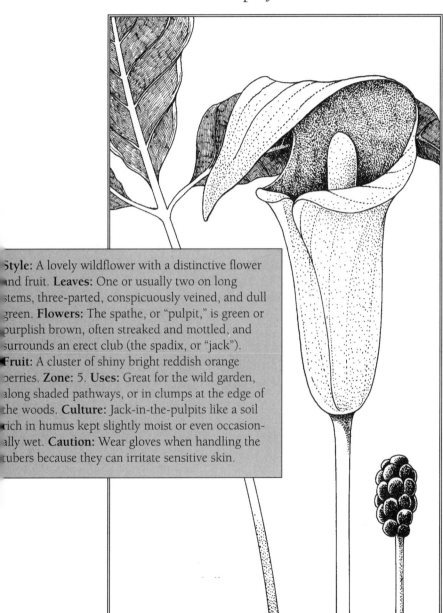

Style: A lovely wildflower with a distinctive flower and fruit. **Leaves:** One or usually two on long stems, three-parted, conspicuously veined, and dull green. **Flowers:** The spathe, or "pulpit," is green or purplish brown, often streaked and mottled, and surrounds an erect club (the spadix, or "jack"). **Fruit:** A cluster of shiny bright reddish orange berries. **Zone:** 5. **Uses:** Great for the wild garden, along shaded pathways, or in clumps at the edge of the woods. **Culture:** Jack-in-the-pulpits like a soil rich in humus kept slightly moist or even occasionally wet. **Caution:** Wear gloves when handling the tubers because they can irritate sensitive skin.

To Flint's Pond. Arum triphyllum *out. Almost every one has a little fly or two concealed within. One of the handsomest-formed plants when in flower. Sorrel out in rain, apparently a day or two. . . . A blue heron flies away from the shore of the pond.* —May 11, 1859

It's strange that Thoreau called this plant *Arum* since that scientific name was replaced with *Arisaema* as the recognized genus by John Torrey in 1843. Not only that, but Thoreau with his great imagination never once called the flower by its common names of Indian turnip and jack-in-the-pulpit. The first is a New World label and the second describes not only the American species but the English wildflower lords-and-ladies or cuckoopint *(Arum maculatum)*, a similar plant known to many settlers of the Northeast.

According to modern references, the scientific name is from the Greek *aris*, an arum, and *aima*, blood, in reference to the red leaves found in certain species. But in *How to Know the Wildflowers*, Mrs. William Starr Dana claims that *Arisaema*, signifying bloody arum, refers to the dark purple stains found on the spathes of the more purple flowers. I prefer her derivation. The species name, *triphyllum*, refers to the three leaflets usually overtopping the spathe.

Although most references use the common name of jack-in-the-pulpit, other common names include bog onion, brown dragon, cuckoo plant (obviously referring to the English plant), memory root (because of the burning produced by eating an unprepared tuber), pepper turnip (for the same reason), petit prêcheur (in Canada), priests pentle, starchwort, and wake robin.

The range of these plants extends from southern Quebec and New Brunswick south through the Appalachians and coastal plain to Florida, then west to Louisiana and eastern Texas.

While many gardeners think of this plant as somewhat small in stature, when sited in rich soil with overhead shade and given plenty of moisture, Indian turnips can become very large and stately.

Stopped to drink at the Hosmer Spring, I saw a hundred
caddis-cases, of light-colored pebbles, at the bottom . . .
apparently on their way to becoming perfect insects. . . .
Under the oak in Brown's moraine pasture, by Water Dock
Meadow, a great arum more than three feet high, like a
tropical plant, in open land, with leaflets more than a foot
long.   *—July 17, 1856*

On a day in June, I went out to the woodland path where a
colony of jacks has appeared over the past few years. Two plants
are just one inch shy of three feet, and the developing berry bunch
is already an inch and a quarter long.

At one time botanists thought that a green spathe surrounded
male flowers and a purple hood contained female flowers. Today
we know that spathe color has no relation to the sex of the blossoms below the hood. Although the plants are unisexual, with the
tiny male or female flowers found at the base of the jack, or spadix,
in separate spathes, sometimes a spathe will contain flowers of
both sexes, but these plants are relatively rare. Some authorities
still recognize three species based on minor differences in the
leaves, the spathes, and the sizes of the plants, but for the sake of
convenience, I'll stick to one.

The flowers are not fertilized by bees, because these hardy insects are off foraging in the sunlit fields close by. Deep within the
woods, pollination is assisted by insects such as fungus gnats, flies,
or beetles.

In *Nature's Garden*, Neltje Blanchan writes about the pollination of jack-in-the-pulpits: "A fungus gnat, enticed perhaps by the
striped house of refuge from cold spring winds, and with a
prospect of food below, enters and slides down the inside walls or
the slippery colored column: in either case descent is very easy; it
is the return that is made so difficult, if not impossible for the tiny
visitor. Squeezing past the projecting ledge [at the base of the
spadix] the gnat finds himself in a roomy apartment whose floor—

the bottom of the pulpit—is dusted over with fine pollen; that is, if he is among staminate flowers already mature."

Now the pollen-covered gnat tries to escape, but the walls are too slippery and its wings keep hitting the projecting ledge above. If the gnat perseveres, it will find one opening—a gap in the fold of the spathe where it meets in the front of the flower—and finally escape to the outside. Once free, the gnat will quickly fly within another flower, but on this trip, pollen will be carried along.

Gnats often become exhausted by the rigors of escape and fall dead to the flower floor, and if you peel open one of jack's pulpits, you will sometimes find the victims.

On September 3, 1856, Thoreau wrote about the jack's berries: "There are many splendid scarlet arum berries there now in prime, forming a dense ovate head on a short peduncle. The individual berries are of various sizes, between pear and mitre and club form, flattened against each other on a singular (now purple and white) core, which is hollow. What rank and venomous luxuriance in this swamp sproutland!"

Some three weeks later on September 28, he made the following entry: "The arum berries are still fresh and abundant, perhaps in their prime. A large cluster is two and a half inches long by two wide and rather flattish. One, which has ripened prematurely, the stalk being withered and drooping, resembles a very short thick ear of scarlet corn. This might well enough be called snake-corn. These singular vermilion-colored berries, about a hundred of them, surmount a purple bag on a peduncle six or eight inches long. It is one of the most remarkable and dazzling, if not the handsomest, fruits we have. These were by violet wood-sorrel wall. How many fruits are scarlet now!"

Thoreau's enthusiasm for jacks never waned; on September 1, 1859, he continued his praise: "The fruit of the arum is the most remarkable that I see this afternoon, such brilliancy, color, and form; perhaps in prime now. It is among the most easily detected now on the floor of the swamp, its bright-scarlet cone above the fallen and withered leaves and amid its own brown or whitish and withering leaves. Its own leaves and stem perhaps soft and decaying, while it is perfectly fresh and dazzling. It has the brightest gloss of any fruit I remember, and this makes the green ones about as remarkable as the scarlet, with, perchance, a part of the withered spathe still investing and veiling it. The scarlet fruit of the arum spots the swamp floor."

Although the berries taste acrid, the real shock comes with tasting the tuber before it is properly prepared. Needlelike crystals of calcium oxalate cause a strong burning sensation if the tuber is eaten raw. Older books claim the American Indians boiled both the bright scarlet berries and the tuber to make them palatable, but Oliver Perry Medsger, in his marvelous book *Edible Wild Plants* (New York: The Macmillan Company, 1966), has different instructions:

"I have experimented with the Indian turnip; after boiling and changing the water two or three times, the roots were still too pungent to eat. When I left them for several weeks, or until they were thoroughly dried, the acrid condition naturally left them and the starch became pleasant and nutritious. . . . Perhaps it would be best to first boil, then dry them; afterward they could be ground into meal and baked into cakes or used for gruel after the Indian fashion."

The American Indians used the dried, aged root to treat colds and hacking coughs and to enrich the blood. Poultices of the root were used to treat rheumatism, scrofulous sores, boils, abscesses, ringworm, and even snakebites. English doctors recommended the root for whooping cough, bronchitis, laryngitis, flatulence, and asthma.

Bebe Miles, writing in *Wildflower Perennials for Your Garden* (Harrisburg: Stackpole Books, 1995), tells how to make the jack "speak": "Gently rub the bottom of the spathe between your fingers, and squeaky noises will entertain your children."

The easiest way to propagate jacks is to collect the ripened fruits when they are brightly colored and plump, squash them open, and plant the seeds outdoors immediately, so that they have a winter in the cold.

Believe it or not, a cultivar of the jack-in-the-pulpit is listed in *Hortus Third:* 'Zebrinum' has a purple spathe with whitish longitudinal stripes on the inside. I've never seen it offered by any nursery.

A NUMBER OF MILKWEEDS
The Common Milkweed
Asclepias syriaca (A. cornuti)

Style: Statuesque field plant up to six feet high with distinctive flowers and fruits, attractive to monarch butterflies. **Leaves:** Four to ten inches long, opposite, light green, exuding a milky sap when broken. **Flowers:** Many half-inch flowers varying from purple to pink, with a conspicuous five-part central crown, growing in clusters two to three inches wide. **Fruit:** Rough-textured pods that split open on one side releasing many overlapping seeds, each connected to a tuft of silky hairs. **Zone:** 5. **Uses:** For the wild or meadow garden. **Culture:** Full sun in well-drained but average soil.

I notice two varieties (?), perhaps, of Asclepias cornuti now out, one on the railroad meadow this side the Brooks Crossing, the other beyond the first mile-post above. The last has broader leaves and blunter and more decidedly mucronate, and pedicels and peduncles quite downy, the former being little more than twice the length of the petals. The other has narrower and more pointed leaves . . .   —July 5, 1856

IN ALL OF THOREAU'S JOURNAL I FOUND NO MORE THAN THE ABOVE PASS-ing (and confusing) reference to the flowers of the common milkweed, but there are pages of documentation on the beauty and utility of the milkweed pod and its seeds. But before the beauty of the seeds comes the fascinating flower.

The common milkweed is known as *Asclepias syriaca* or, in older books, *A. cornuti*. The genus name honors the mythic Greek physician Aesculapius, son of Apollo and Coronis, who was killed by Zeus when he became so proficient in healing that he revived the dead. As to the present species name, *syriaca*, Linnaeus mistakenly thought the original plant came from Syria. *Cornuti*, a name honoring Jacques Cornut, who in 1635 described forty Canadian plants in his *Historia Canadensium Plantarum*, is by far the better choice. But the rules state that the first name given to a plant, regardless of how inappropriate it is, must be used. Over the last few centuries many names have changed and as historical investigations continue, many more will probably fall to this rule.

The way in which the flowers of the milkweed ensure pollination is outdone only by the sometimes Machiavellian adaptations of the orchid family. When you watch the blossoms of the common milkweed, be prepared for high drama.

The rich fragrance and color of the flowers attract not only butterflies but also wasps, flies, beetles, and bees. Upon arrival the insect visitors find that the flower's surface is slick and they must claw about in order to gain a foothold; all this activity is part of a plan. As the insects struggle, one or more of the sharp projections on their feet will catch in little clefts at the flower's base. Soon a foot is drawn into a slot at the end of which is a little dark brown container that holds masses of yellow pollen. The pollen container is very hard and has a notch in its face that hooks itself to insect feet. When a visitor gives that final, necessary tug to free itself, the container goes along, firmly caught until the insect lands on another flower, where the pollen container may fall through a slot and fertilize the flower.

This mechanism doesn't always work to the flower's advantage (nor the insect's). Upon examining milkweed flowers, you will often find small insects trying to escape but to no avail. Spiders, ants, and beetles use these flowers as hunting grounds, so nothing goes to waste. Bumblebees are large and heavy enough to avoid being caught in these pollination devices, and small butterflies are so light footed that they can feed but never get trapped. It is large butterflies like swallowtails and monarchs that escape from the traps and carry the pollen to other flowers.

I hesitate to quote Neltje Blanchan's instructions on setting the milkweed flower mechanism to work because of possible action by the Fly Protection League, but here goes:

"If you have neither time nor patience to sit in the hot sun, magnifying-glass in hand, and watch for an unwary insect to get caught, take an ordinary housefly, and hold it by the wings so that it may claw at one of the newly opened flowers from which no pollinia have been removed. It tries frantically to hold on, and with a little direction it may be let to catch its claws in the slots of the flower. Now pull it gently away, and you will find a pair of saddle-bags slung over his foot by a slender curved stalk. If you are rarely skillful, you may induce your fly to withdraw the pollinia from all five slots on as many of his feet. And they are not to be thrown or scraped off, let the fly try as hard as he pleases. You may now invite the fly to take a walk on another flower in which he will probably leave one or more pollinia in its stigmatic cavities."

On a beautiful early autumn day, Thoreau visited Clematis Brook, where he noted the following:

The pods or follicles of the Asclepias syriaca *now point upward. Did they before all point down? Have they turned up? They are already bursting. I release some seeds with the long, fine silk attached. The fine threads fly apart at once, open with a spring, and they ray themselves out into a hemispherical form, each thread freeing itself from its neighbor and all reflecting prismatic or rainbow tints. The seeds, besides, are furnished with wings, which plainly keep them steady and prevent their whirling round. I let one go, and it rises slowly and uncertainly at first, now driven this way, then that, by currents which I cannot perceive, and I fear it will make shipwreck against the neighboring wood; but no, as it approaches it, it surely rises above it, and then, feeling the north wind, it is borne off rapidly in the opposite direction, ever rising higher and higher and tossing and heaved about with every fluctuation of the air, till, at a hundred feet above the earth and fifty rods off, steering south, I lose sight of it. How many myriads go sailing away at this season, high over hill and meadow and river, on various tacks until the wind lulls, to plant their race in new localities, who can tell how many miles distant! And for this end these silken streamers have been perfecting all summer, snugly packed in this light chest,—a perfect adaptation to this end, a prophecy not only of the fall but of future springs. Who could believe in prophecies of Daniel or of Miller that the world would end this summer, while one milkweed with faith matured its seeds?*

I watched the seeds of the milkweed rising higher and higher till lost in the sky, with as much interest as his friends did Mr. Lauriat. I brought home two of the pods which were already bursting open, and amused myself from day to day with releasing the seeds and watching [them] rise slowly into the heavens till they were lost to my eye. No doubt the greater or less rapidity with which they rose would serve as a natural barometer to test the conditions of the air.

—*September 25, 1851*

Only one question came to my mind when reading this passage, and that concerned Mr. Lauriat. I could find no reference to this gentleman, but from the description, I assume he was a balloonist of note.

Earlier, in August of that same year, Thoreau described talking with the family's Irish washwoman, who, when she saw him playing with milkweed seeds, told him that back in Ireland people filled beds with that down. But he also noted that milkweeds are not indigenous to Europe. It's possible that she confused milkweed fluff with thistle fluff, since they both have the same uses.

Then, in October, when winter was not too far around the corner, Thoreau noted the following:

> Goldfinches are in the air. I hear a blackbird also, and see a downy woodpecker, and see and hear a hairy one. The seeds of the pasture thistle are not so buoyed up by their down as the milkweed. . . . The milkweed seeds must be carried far, for it is only when a strong wind is blowing that they are loosened from their pods.   —October 9, 1851

Seven years later Thoreau wrote again about the flying silken seeds:

> Near the end of the causeway, milkweed is copiously discounting. This is much fairer than the thistle down. It apparently bursts its pods after rain especially (as yesterday's), opening on the under side, away from succeeding rains. Half a dozen seeds or more, attached by the tips of their silks to the core of the pod, will be blown about there a long time before a strong puff launches them away, and in the meanwhile they are expanding and drying their silk.   —October 25, 1858

As a foodstuff, milkweed plants can be collected when they are young and tender, only about a few inches high. Wash them thoroughly, then boil the sprouts, changing the water a few times to remove the milky juice. When cooked well milkweed tastes like spinach. In Canada, these same tender stems are eaten like asparagus.

American Indians made a root tea used both as a laxative and as a diuretic for kidney stones. They also used the latex sap to treat both warts and ringworm. Early American doctors treated asthma and rheumatism with milkweed preparations. The latex was often chewed as a gum, but common milkweed is potentially toxic and this use should always be discouraged.

The Quebec Indians used milkweed as a contraceptive because an infusion of pounded roots was said to induce temporary sterility in women.

The silky hairs of the seeds have been used for the stuffing of pillows and mattresses and can be mixed with flax or wool and woven into various textiles; even paper has been manufactured from this fluff. During the Second World War, milkweed floss was gathered by schoolchildren in burlap sacks and used as a substitute for kapok in the manufacture of Mae West life preservers for both the navy and air force. Scientific work to develop milkweed latex as a rubber substitute was abandoned at the war's end.

There is a beneficial relationship between monarch butterflies (*Danaus plexippus*) and the common milkweed. Besides pollinating the flowers, monarchs lay their eggs on milkweeds. When hatched, the caterpillars feed on the leaves, which contain cardiac glycosides that are somewhat similar to digitalin used in the treatment of heart disease. When these chemicals are absorbed by the butterfly larvae, whose sole source of food is milkweed foliage, they become toxic to birds and other predators. The black-and-orange pattern of the adult monarch's wings continues to warn enemies of the noxious taste of these butterflies.

The Swamp Milkweed
Asclepias incarnata

I am entering Fair Haven Pond. It is now perfectly still and smooth, like dark glass. Yet the westering sun is very warm. He who passes over a lake at noon, when the waves run, little imagines its serene and placid beauty at evening, as little as he anticipates his own serenity. There is no more beautiful part of the river than the entrance to this pond. The Asclepias incarnata *is well named water silkweed, for it grows here amid the button-bushes and willows in the wettest places along the river.*

—July 20, 1853

Style: A smaller milkweed, usually between four and five feet high, that is more suited to the garden proper. **Leaves:** Four inches long, smooth and lance shaped, opposite, with a somewhat milky sap. **Flowers:** Many quarter-inch, deep pink flowers in small clusters about two inches wide. **Fruit:** An elongated pod from two to four inches long, opening on one side and releasing many overlapping seeds, each connected to a tuft of silky hairs. **Zone:** 5. **Uses:** Great for the wild garden, meadow garden, and the back of the border. **Culture:** Full sun in moist, even wet, soil.

The water milkweed is an interesting red, here and there, like roses along the shore.   —August 5, 1858

THOREAU CALLED THE SWAMP MILKWEED THE WATER MILKWEED, AND HE noted the color of the flowers, a color so grand that it makes the plant a necessary addition to the wild garden or the garden border. Few nurseries carry this beautiful plant. They think, I suppose, that the word "swamp" will turn off the gardening public, giving gardeners the message that swamp milkweeds won't succeed unless bullfrogs croak and giant roots of sunken cypresses are reflected in muddy waters just outside their door.

Butterfly-weed
Asclepias tuberosa

Style: A demure milkweed with dozens of bright orange flower clusters on plants never more than three feet tall. **Leaves:** Three to six inches long, alternate, and very narrow, with a watery juice, not a milky sap. **Flowers:** Many three-eighth-inch flowers of bright orange in two-inch clusters. **Fruit:** Spindle-shaped, narrow, hairy, erect pods releasing seeds connected to tufts of silky hairs. **Zone:** 5. **Uses:** Great for the wild garden, meadow garden, and the garden proper. **Culture:** Full sun in well-drained but average soil.

THOREAU NEVER MENTIONED THIS MILK-weed. Perhaps when he was writing the journal, the plant hadn't yet wandered east to Walden, but I'm surprised, and sorry, that he missed it. In addition to the common name of butterfly-weed, this member of the family is also called pleurisy-root, yellow milkweed, and chigger-flower. Its range is from New Hampshire to Minnesota and Colorado and southward to Florida, Texas, and Arizona. Here in western North Carolina, it grows in ditches along the sides of country roads and at the margin between the woods and the open fields.

Easily started from seed, in a few years one plant will become a sizable clump producing masses of the bright orange flowers. Because they eventually produce a sizable root system, the plants are both resistant to drought and difficult to move, so only transplant small specimens. In the wild these plants grow in the poorest of soils, so when given good, well-drained garden soil, they soon are larger than those in the field but never need staking.

Check the seed catalogs for new-color cultivars. English gardeners have been quick to introduce new shades. The cultivar 'Gay Butterflies Mixed' produces shades of scarlet, gold, and pink, some bicolors, and the more common orange.

William H. Frederick, Jr., author of *The Exuberant Garden and the Controlling Hand* (Boston: Little, Brown and Company, 1992), designed a garden that included thirty-six black-eyed Susans (*Rudbeckia fulgida* var. *Sullivantii* 'Goldsturm') and forty-eight butterfly-weeds set among meadow grasses. The effect is pure delight!

Once they bloom you will immediately understand where the most popular common name came from. Swallowtails, fritillaries, monarchs, yellow sulfurs, painted ladies, and bronze coppers will all come to visit these flowers. If grown in your garden, what Thoreau termed "that meager assemblage of curiosities, that poor apology for Nature and Art which I call my front yard," butterfly-weeds will add both style and substance.

The American Indians used the large, tuberous roots for lung inflammations, asthma, and bronchitis. A root poultice was used to treat swellings, rheumatism, and bruises. Like other milkweeds, butterfly-weed is potentially toxic.

THE ASTERS
Aster spp.

Style: Starlike flowers of late summer and fall blooming in a profusion of blues, whites, and pastels, usually on tall plants with strong stems. **Leaves:** Simple, alternate, sometimes toothed. **Flowers:** Best described as little daisies with varying numbers of petals that are really called rays. **Zone:** 3. **Uses:** Grown in both wild and civilized gardens. **Culture:** Tolerant of most conditions but do best in an average soil in full sun, although some species will do well in wooded shade.

Aster novae-angliae

I go to Walden via the almshouse and up the railroad. Trees seen in the east against the dark cloud, the sun shining on them, are perfectly white as frostwork, and their outlines very perfectly and distinctly revealed, great wisps that they are and ghosts of trees, with recurved twigs. The walls and fences are encased, and the fields bristle with a myriad of crystal spears. Already the wind is rising and a brattling is heard overhead in the street. The sun, shining down a gorge over the woods at Brister's Hill, reveals a wonderfully brilliant as well as seemingly solid and diversified region in the air. The ice is from an eighth to a quarter of an inch thick about the twigs and pine needles . . . and needles are stiff, as if preserved under glass for the inspection of posterity. . . . But the low and spreading weeds in the fields and the wood-paths are the most interesting. Here are asters, savory-leaved, whose flat imbricated calyxes, three quarters of an inch over, are surmounted and inclosed in a perfectly transparent ice button, like a glass knob, through which you see the reflections of the brown calyx. . . . Each little blue-curls calyx has a spherical button like those brass ones on little boys' jackets,—little sprigs on them,—and the pennyroyal has still smaller spheres, more regularly arranged around the stem, chandelier-wise, and still smells through the ice. —December 26, 1855

The genus *Aster* derives from the Greek word *aster,* or star. The flower's central disk contains the true flowers, tiny tubes full of nectar and dusted with pollen, whereas the so-called petals are really the ray flowers, their lovely colors meant to attract insects. You need a hand lens to really see just how many flowers there are in that disk and the marvelous mathematical arrangement to which they conform. Common names for asters include Michaelmas daisy, starwort, and frostflower. Most of the species are native to much of the United States, reaching up into Canada and down to the Southwest.

An *Illustrated Flora of the Northern United States, Canada, and the British Possessions,* by Nathaniel Lord Britton and Addison Brown (New York: Charles Scribner's Sons, 1898), lists over two hundred species and subspecies of the genus *Aster.* Throughout a bewildering array of botanical descriptions, the authors rarely editorialized, but they did describe the New England aster (*Aster novae-angliae*) as "one of the most beautiful of the genus." And it is. Asters seem to glow underneath the autumn sun, turning the surrounding slightly summer-burned grasses to becoming frames for floral splendor.

In late August 1853, as he walked to Bidens Brook, Thoreau wrote about the bewildering beauty and variety of the asters that were all in full bloom. He mentioned *Aster laevis,* a large and handsome species with various leaf shapes; *A. patens,* known for its small, blunt leaves and ray flowers ranging from pink to violet; and *A. linearifolius,* the bristle-starred aster. This last species is rarely more than two feet high and is considered one of the more beautiful asters. The profusion of flowers led Thoreau to ask, "Why so many asters and goldenrods now? The sun has shone on the earth, and the goldenrod is his fruit. The stars, too, have shone on it, and the asters are their fruit."

During the first week of September 1853, Thoreau went for a long walk along the turnpike and returned by Goose Pond, collecting along the way twelve species of asters, which he placed in a pail full of water. After arranging them side by side, he and his sister, Sophia, judged *Aster patens,* with its large, deep purple flowers, as the handsomest, at the same time pointing out that *A. tradescantii* attracted attention in a vase, with its often perfect hollow pyramids of flowers with yellow or purplish disks.

The following week, just before his second trip to the Maine woods, Thoreau was struck by the beauty of the wood aster, *Aster corymbosus* (today known as *A. divaricatus*), "with its corymbed flowers, its seven or eight long slender white rays pointed at both ends, ready to curl, shaving-like, and purplish disks,—one of the more interesting asters."

On September 1, 1856, Thoreau made a list of twelve species of asters, including *Aster patens* ("apparently now in prime and the most abundant of the larger asters"), *Aster laevis* ("just beginning"), and the heath aster, today named *Aster ericoides* but at that time called *A. multiflorus* ("not one seen yet").

Then on September 24, he did it again, listing thirteen species, noting that most were in their prime. Finally, on October 8, he again gives the listing, but now the general comment is that they "are probably nearly done."

Although throughout the journals there are countless references to the asters, always pointing out their beauty and their abundance, there is never a mention of the New England aster, *Aster novae-angliae,* or the New York aster, *A. novi-belgii.*

The New England aster is one of the parents used to produce a strain of garden hybrids that blooms from mid-September to frost. The species will often reach six feet, but the cultivars stay at five feet or below. 'Harrington's Pink' has medium-sized soft salmon pink flowers on stems about forty inches high; the beautiful 'Alma Potschke' wears warm pink flowers on three-foot stems that bloom for at least six weeks. Cutting the taller varieties back halfway just before midsummer will bring more compact blooming. This is the only wild aster known for its medicinal uses. The American Indians made a root tea for the treatment of diarrhea and fevers.

The New York aster runs along the East Coast from Newfoundland to Georgia, especially on the ocean shore, in meadows, and in damp thickets. Unlike the New England varieties, the New Yorkers rarely top three feet. The species name is Latin for "of New Belgium," an early name for New York. The usual flower colors are violet blue rays surrounding yellow—or sometimes reddish—disk flowers. Hybrids of *A. novi-belgii* and *A. dumosus* produce compact mounds of flowers never topping sixteen inches. 'Schneekissen' is pure white, 'Lady in Blue' is a semidouble of powder blue, and 'Kassel' bears carmine red flowers.

Thoreau did write about *Aster tradescantii* on a number of

occasions and described it as having half-inch white flowers borne on leafy stems to twenty-four inches high. "With yellow disks turning reddish or purplish, [it] is very pretty by the low roadsides, resounding with the hum of honeybees; [and] commonly despised for its smallness and commonness,—with crowded systems of little suns." In 1633 that particular aster was the first American species to be imported to Europe by John Tradescant, whose father was gardener to King Charles I.

The heath aster (*Aster ericoides*), a plant reaching a height of four feet, has narrow, stiff leaves (that liken it to erica, or heath), bears numerous, small flower heads about an eighth inch high, and is so covered with blossoms that it's a most attractive addition to the garden. Hybridizers have produced a cultivar, 'Golden Spray', a twenty-four-inch plant with golden flowers and attractive foliage.

Among the choice species asters, *Aster divaricatus*, the white wood aster, is a shade tolerant plant found from New Hampshire, west to Ohio, and south to Georgia. *Aster cordifolius*, or the blue wood aster, is perfect in light shade. But to my mind, the big awards go to *A. lateriflorus*, the calico or starved aster (the second description due to the visible stems). Represented in the trade by 'Horizontalis', this four-foot plant bears tiny panicles of lilac flowers blooming above horizontal, leafy branches that turn coppery purple for fall. The calico aster was not introduced into English gardens until 1829.

Finally, we should note the existence of two other asters that Thoreau missed. The showy or seaside purple aster (*Aster spectabilis*) grows to about two feet, with bladelike leaves and bright, violet purple flower heads that have individual flowers about an inch and a half across. This species was taken to England in 1777 and was featured in the nursery trade by 1789.

The second oversight, basically a southern plant, is *Aster carolinianus*, the autumn-flowered climbing aster. Climbing asters are unusual composite vines or, perhaps, robust sprawling perennials.

They have been used to great effect in the Early-Late Border of the North Carolina State University Arboretum at Raleigh, where Edith Eddleman allows the rambling stems to climb through the branches of an American beautyberry (*Callicarpa americana*) for a spectacular fall display. By early October, masses of one-inch purple flowers shine against the background of beautyberry fruit. References give the plant's height at six feet in nature, but garden observations have recorded plants reaching twelve to fifteen feet. The arboretum suggests its possible use in hanging baskets for autumn color, or because plants bloom photoperiodically, cued by short days in the fall, it could be bedded out in spring as an annual in colder climates.

To become involved with the aster family is to embark on a lifelong career of beauty coupled with confusion. Some groups are almost impossible to classify unless you are a trained botanist. There are hundreds of species in our woods, and like the goldenrods, they have a tendency to interbreed, producing hybrids that only confuse the already disorderly characteristics. If serious about identifications, whatever your approach to gardening, make sure you carry a good hand lens.

The aster genus is characterized by floral bracts that overlap in several circles; the rays (or petals) are purple, lavender, pink, blue, or white; and the disks contain very small yellow flowers that in some species have a reddish cast.

THE COMMON OR EUROPEAN BARBERRY
Berberis vulgaris

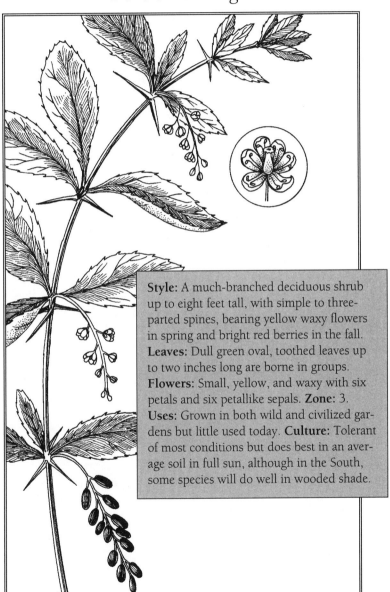

Style: A much-branched deciduous shrub up to eight feet tall, with simple to three-parted spines, bearing yellow waxy flowers in spring and bright red berries in the fall. **Leaves:** Dull green oval, toothed leaves up to two inches long are borne in groups. **Flowers:** Small, yellow, and waxy with six petals and six petallike sepals. **Zone:** 3. **Uses:** Grown in both wild and civilized gardens but little used today. **Culture:** Tolerant of most conditions but does best in an average soil in full sun, although in the South, some species will do well in wooded shade.

*The barberry blossoms are now abundant. They fill the air
with a disagreeable, buttery fragrance.   —June 2, 1852*

I've always liked barberries and it turns out that, notwithstanding the above statement, Thoreau did, too. Although the yellow flowers of the common barberry do have a disagreeable smell, the plant more than makes up for this minor flaw with a number of positive traits.

That's why it's good that Thoreau's Garden is a garden of the mind. The small pool is kept full by a waterfall that ripples along, fed by a hidden spring, glistening as it turns and tumbles over rocks. Perfect ferns arch over the pool and everything is shaded by a towering three-hundred-year-old tulip tree. And there's a comfortable rush chair that is impervious to the elements, a chair for dreaming and thinking, a chair for idleness. Surrounding this garden is an impermeable hedge of common barberry, protecting me from the world, just as in ages past hedges ringed farms to keep out the wild.

Because of both its thorns and its medicinal uses, barberry has been an English tradition since medieval times. Cloister gardens used by both monks and nuns were protected by these shrubs. According to Sir John Mandeville (a pseudonym for a fourteenth-century French physician who wrote about his travels to Arabia, India, and China), Christ's crown of thorns had four circlets, each made of a different spiny plant, one of them barberry. And because its thorns grow in threes, the plant could represent the Trinity.

The genus name is derived from the word *berberys,* the Arabian name of the fruit. A few references maintain that the plants are named in honor of St. Barbara, the patron saint of firearms (an honor bestowed upon Barbara after she was beheaded by her father for being a Christian, and he was then consumed in thunder and lightning). I've never found the reason for her name being associated with the plant. Some of the other common names for the barberry used over the centuries include the guild tree, woodour, woodsore, and the pipperidge bush, a name of uncertain derivation.

Before doing research for this book, I was unaware that growing the common barberry (*Berberis vulgaris*) could present a problem. It turns out that barberry leaves serve as hosts to one of the stages in the life cycle of the fungus *Puccinia graminis*, the cause of a devastating disease in wheat called wheat rust. Over the course of many years, the basic solution offered for fighting this rust was to eradicate all the barberries you could find rather than simply stop growing barberries in the vicinity of wheat fields. Many U.S. states and European nations adopted programs to eliminate the plants. In France and Germany, for example, laws ordered the destruction of the common barberry, even though many climates where barberries grew were not suitable to the formation of the disease spores. According to L. H. Bailey, "destroying the barberry will not check the fungus, as it can grow and spread for years without entering the stage where barberry acts as the host." But destroy it they did, and by 1865, at the height of the rust panic, the common barberry was almost eliminated.

That barberry bush near the bars on Conantum is methinks now the most beautiful, light, and graceful bush that I ever saw in bloom. It is shaped like a haycock, broad and dense, yet light as if some leaven had raised it. But how orientally beautiful now, seen through this dark mizzling air, its parallel or rather concentric wreaths composed of leaves and flowers keeping each other apart and lightening the whole mass, each wreath above composed of rich dark-green leaves, below of drooping racemes of lively yellow flowers! Its beauty consists in a great measure in this intimate mixture of flowers and leaves, the small rich-colored flowers not being too much massed. It suggests the yellow-robed priests perchance of Tibet. The lowest wreaths lie on the ground. But go not so near as to be disturbed by that sickening buttery odor, as of an underdone batter pudding, all eggs but no spice. Who would think this would bake into such a red acid fruit? —May 1853

There's that smell again. Mildly unpleasant, it's rather like the foxy smell of boxwood: some people are disturbed by it; others pay it no mind. Louise Beebe Wilder notes that "the odor of [barberries] which close at hand is somewhat overpowering, [is] pleasant enough when borne on a wandering breeze from a little distance." The English gardener Gertrude Jekyll is of a different opinion. "There was one flower smell," she wrote, "that I always thought odious, that of the common barberry. After a time when I learnt how the wind carries scent I used to approach it cautiously from the windward side. The smell is not really very bad but of a faint and sickly kind but I remember years when to me it was so odious that it inspired me with a sort of fear, and when I forgot that the barberries were near and walked into the smell without expecting it, I used to run away as fast as I could in a kind of terror." Believe me, it's not that bad!

When he noted that the flower color matches that of the silken robes worn by Tibetan priests, Thoreau was not far wrong. A friend of mine enjoyed having a Tibetan priest as a house guest earlier this year and the yellow of his robes was quite close to the color of the common barberry flower.

Two journal entries deal with picking barberries:

The barberries are not wholly reddened yet. How much handsomer in fruit for being bent down in wreaths by the weight! The increasing weight of the fruits adds gracefulness to the form of the bush. I get my hands full of thorns, but my basket full of berries. How productive a barberry bush! On each the berries seem more abundant and plumper than on the last. —September 18, 1854

We got about three pecks of barberries from four or five bushes, but I filled my fingers with prickles to pay for them. With the hands well defended, it would be pleasant picking, they are so handsome, and beside are so abundant and fill

*up so fast. I take hold of the end of the drooping twigs with
my left hand, raise them, and then strip downward at once
as many clusters as my hand will embrace, commonly bring
away with the raceme two small green leaves or bracts,
which I do not stop to pick out. When I come to a particularly thick and handsome wreath of fruit, I pluck the twig
entire and bend it around the inside of the basket. Some
bushes bear much larger and plumper berries than others.
Some also are comparatively green yet. Meanwhile the cat-
bird mews in the alders by my side, and the scream of the
jay is heard from the wood-side.   —September 24, 1855*

About a year later, barberries were mentioned again. After he
had carefully gathered a full peck of berries from three bushes, he
called himself the best barberry picker. But he noted that, for all
his knack, a pair of gloves would be a good idea because it would
be many days before he could remove all the prickles from his
tortured fingers.

Why was Thoreau gathering berries? Because until the last
century barberry fruits were collected to make jams and jellies
and preserved in vinegar, used to complement both meat and fish.
John Parkinson (1567–1650), writing in *A Garden of Pleasant
Flowers,* thought they were a good appetizer "for those that loath
their meate," and according to herbalist Nicholas Culpeper
(1616–1654), "They get a man a good stomach to his victuals by
strengthening the attractive faculty which is under Mars." I can
remember my mother talking about barberry jelly—she said it was
superior to barberry jam—but I cannot remember her actually
making it. Although the berries are edible fresh, they are extremely
sour.

According to Alice M. Coats in *Garden Shrubs and Their His-
tories* (New York: Simon and Schuster, 1992), the fruit was still
being gathered for the table in 1863, at which time five different
varieties were available. Not only were the berries used but the

leaves were also employed to make a sour sauce like that made from sorrel. Remember that in 1865 the rust panic was at its height, and that might have been partly responsible for the berries' decline.

> *I think that the bright-yellow wood of the barberry, which I have occasion to break in my surveying, is the most interesting and remarkable for its color.* —*January 12, 1857*

(After the publication of *Walden,* Thoreau turned to the job of surveying, an occupation that allowed him to be out and about but not tied down to any special routine.)

According to the Doctrine of Signatures (a medieval philosophy of medicine whereby a plant's physical appearance revealed its therapeutic benefits), the inner bark of the common barberry, being yellow, was good for treating jaundice, hence another common name—the jaundice bush. Parkinson suggested boiling the inner bark or the roots in ale or other drinks as a treatment for that disease. The bark was also used to make both a clothing and a hair dye. Barberry wood was used to make small wooden objects, especially toothpicks, because it resisted splitting. The early settlers, who brought the plant over from Europe, made a berry tea for the treatment of poor appetite and for use as an expectorant and a laxative. A root-bark tea was used to promote sweating, and a tincture made from root bark was used to treat arthritis, rheumatism, and sciatica. The whole plant contains berberine, a chemical with possible application as a bacterial inhibitor. But current books contain warnings about its use.

To round out the barberry story, we return to the flowers. There are six stamens in a barberry blossom, each capped by an anther described as a little pollen box with a trapdoor on either side. Each stamen is like a hair trigger on a pistol: when touched by an insect it reacts like the wire in a mousetrap, breaking open the trapdoor (a onetime happening) and showering the insect with pollen. The action of the barberry stamen led to the belief that the flowers possessed a primitive nervous system. Scottish botanist John Claudius Loudon actually treated the plants with arsenic and found that the stamens lost their ability to move. But if he used narcotics like belladonna or opium, the stamens became so flaccid they could be bent at will.

Because of their ample fruit, barberries will seed about. And not only birds are responsible for their wanderings.

> *I mistook dense groves of little barberries in the droppings of cows in the Boulder Field for apple trees at first. So the cows eat barberries, and help disperse or disseminate them exactly as they do the apple! That helps account for the spread of the barberry, then.* —May 29, 1858

There are a few common barberry cultivars, including the purple-leaved 'Atropurpurea' and a form known as 'Variegata', described by Christopher Lloyd as having glossy foliage handsomely splashed with yellow that, unlike many variegated plants, is passed on to the seedlings. English books also mention the yellow-fruited 'Lutea' and 'Macrocarpa', a cultivar with red fruit up to a half inch long.

William Robinson suggests growing the common barberry in company with *Berberis aristata* (or more likely *B. floribunda*), the berries of which are covered with a plumlike white bloom, and the Japanese barberry (*B. thunbergii*), which has beautiful scarlet berries that remain on the bush throughout the fall.

The American barberry (*Berberis canadensis*) is a deciduous, spiny shrub that grows to six feet and bears scarlet fruit. Its home is in the Allegheny Mountains in Virginia, south to Georgia, and then west to Missouri.

THE CARDOON
Cynara cardunculus

Style: A large silver plant with great presence and big thistle-like blooms. **Leaves:** Deeply cut and divided, gray-green above and whitish tomentose beneath. **Flowers:** Big purplish blue thistles. **Zone:** 6, with protection. **Uses:** The blanched stems are eaten; plants are big and bold in the garden. **Culture:** Good, well-drained garden soil in full sun; this plant likes lime.

When you get into the road, though far from the town, and feel the sand under your feet, it is as if you had reached your own gravel walk. You no longer hear the whip-poor-will, nor regard your shadow, for here you expect a fellow-traveler. You catch yourself walking merely. The road leads your steps and thoughts alike to the town. You see only the path, and your thoughts wander from the objects which are presented to your senses. You are no longer in place. It is like conformity,—walking in the ways of men. —June 11, 1851

Thoreau was a traveler who, rather than sail the seas or walk the deserts, used his mind's eye to see the sights of the world, often in response to reading the works of others.

On June 11, 1851, Thoreau mentioned reading Darwin's book *Voyage of a Naturalist Around the World,* in which the scientist wrote of his experiences aboard the HMS *Beagle,* a long trip that began on December 27, 1831. "[Darwin] speaks," wrote Thoreau, "of the fennel and the cardoon *(Cynara cardunculus),* introduced from Europe, now very common in those parts of South America."

Cardoons. I had not thought about cardoons since I mentioned them in a lecture to a women's garden club in upstate New York. When I talked about the process of blanching, the ladies did the blanching, their piercing looks telling me that their pampered hands would never be directly involved in doing anything to a vegetable, except moving it—impaled on silver forks—to their painted mouths.

On September 19, 1832, Darwin described how common the cardoon was: "Near the Guardia we find the southern limit of two European plants, now become extraordinarily common. The fennel in great profusion covers the ditch-banks in the neighborhood of Buenos Aires, Monte Video, and other towns. But the cardoon *(Cynara cardunculus)* has a far wider range. . . . I saw it in unfrequented spots in Chile, Entre Rios, and Banda Oriental [a rocky region around the Colorado River in the western part of the country]. In the latter country alone, very many (probably several hundred) square miles are covered by one mass of these prickly plants, and are impenetrable by man or beast. Over the undulating plains, where these great beds occur, nothing else can now live. Before their introduction, however, the surface must have supported, as in other parts, a rank herbage. I doubt whether any case is on record of an invasion on so grand a scale of one plant over the aborigines. As I have already said, I nowhere saw the cardoon south of the Salado; but it is probable that in proportion as that country becomes inhabited, the cardoon will extend its limits."

Darwin mentioned that botanists of the mid-1800s agreed that the cardoon and the artichoke were varieties of one plant. He also stated that an intelligent farmer assured him that he (the farmer) had observed some artichokes changing into the common cardoon in a deserted garden.

At sunrise on the morning of September 21, Darwin's party rode slowly across the Argentine wilderness: "There were immense beds of the thistle, as well as of the cardoon: the whole country, indeed, may be called one great bed of these plants. The two kinds grow separate, each plant in company with its own kind. The cardoon is as high as a horse's back, but the Pampas thistle is often higher than the crown of the rider's head."

Today we know that two species of the eleven found in the genus *Cynara* are grown in the garden: *C. cardunculus,* or cardoon, and *C. scolymus,* the globe or French artichoke, thought by many botanists to be derived from cardoon. The word *cardoon* is from the French word for thistle, *cardone,* and the Italian *cardone* and *carduus,* Latin words for thistle.

Arriving in the early 1500s, the Spanish eventually brought the plants to the first settlement, an area near the city of Buenos Aires, where the dried cardoon flowers were used to curdle milk when making cheese. From there, as Darwin noted, the plants extended their limits.

In *Color in Your Garden,* Penelope Hobhouse notes that cardoons "make bold architectural shapes of dull silver, magnificent as corner features," and William Robinson maintains that artichokes make a foliage plant of great beauty, "especially suitable for the rougher parts of pleasure grounds, grass, etc., which are often occupied by fine plants far less handsome." Graham Stuart Thomas, a man with more green in his thumb than most so-called experts have in their entire hand, calls the cardoon "one of the most magnificent of all herbaceous plants. The leaves alone would warrant its inclusion in any large garden."

When new, cardoon leaves exhibit a downy, whitish gray bottom surface and are gray-green above. They look like a thistle leaf without sharp points and fan out from a ribbed stem that closely resembles a stalk of celery. Given good soil, plenty of water while growing, and a long season, cardoons should reach six feet by summer's end. One plant can be a focal point, standing out with regal splendor from other plants scattered about, and if you have the garden room, a row of these beauties will make a large and formidable hedge.

To top it off, in midsummer the flowers appear. Looking like small artichokes, they are obviously thistles of a sort, bearing many individual purple-blue flowers and spines around the blossoms that are *sharp.* Flowering continues to the end of October and plants withstand frost to at least 28° F. Cardoons are hardy to 0° F when mulched.

Although grown as perennials in Europe and England, in our northern garden of USDA Zone 5, cardoons are treated as annuals. The seeds are started with bottom heat, about six weeks before the last spring frost, and are planted out at the end of May. Cardoons need room to grow, so allow a thirty-six-inch circle for each plant.

Just before the first frosts of autumn, on a bright sunny day when the plants are dry, draw the leaves together around the stem and tie them in place with garden twine. Then take strips of paper about six inches wide and, starting at the bottom, wind them around the leaves right up to the top. If you live in an area with very chilly autumns, tie a three-inch-thick band of hay over the paper for added insulation. Or if available, you can use a large cardboard tube. Ignore this natural sculpture for about a month, at which time the blanching is complete. Plants can also be dug up and planted in a dark, frost-free cellar or garage, where the stems will blanch naturally.

Even without blanching, the tender stalks and the root are used in soups, the tough outer strings being discarded. My Italian friends have informed me that *carduni* are also cut into pieces six inches long, partially boiled in lemon water, dipped in seasoned bread crumbs, and then pan fried. Cardoon slices can also be layered with Parmesan and butter, baked, and then topped with cinnamon.

American garden writers, notably Norman Taylor, thought the leafstalks somewhat bitter and decided that as a vegetable, cardoons were second-class. Mr. Taylor probably liked good old American cooking with plenty of mashed potatoes and gravy, topped off with Jell-O for dessert. More adventuresome cooks have delighted in the bittersweet flavor.

Cardoons have naturalized in parts of three counties in South Carolina, where the flowers are harvested, dried, and sold as "luck" flowers or cardone puffs, often dyed in bright colors and sold to tourists—usually from the North.

THE JIMSONWEED
Datura stramonium

Other comon names: Thorn apple, Jamestown weed, stramonium, devil's trumpet. **Style:** Beautiful flowers on an unattractive annual that is quite dangerous. **Leaves:** Alternate, large, and unpleasant smelling, the edges irregularly wavy-toothed. **Flowers:** Large and showy, about four inches long, and shaped like a funnel with five pointed tips; petals usually white but sometimes a pale lavender. **Fruit:** A strange and prickly egg-shaped capsule, densely packed with seeds. **Uses:** Very decorative but must be treated with care; may possibly be used as a lure to flea beetles since they are drawn to the leaves. **Culture:** It will grow almost anywhere.

We have yet to discover our anodynes and our emetics, although we abound in bitters, astringents, aromatics, and demulcents. In the present state of our knowledge we could not well dispense with opium and ipecacuanha, yet a great number of foreign drugs, such as gentian, columbo, chamomile, kino, catechu, cascarilla, canella, etc., for which we pay a large annual tax to other countries, might in all probability be superseded by the indigenous products of our own. It is certainly better that in our own country people should have the benefit of collecting such articles, than that we should pay for them to the Moors of Africa, or the Indians of Brazil.

The thorn apple (Datura stramonium) (apple of Peru, devil's-apple, Jamestown-weed) "emigrates with great facility, and often springs up in the ballast of ships, and in earth carried from one country to another." It secrets itself in the hold of vessels and migrates. It is a sort of cosmopolitan weed, a roving weed. What adventures! What historian knows when first it came into a country! He quotes Beverly's "History of Virginia" as saying that some soldiers in the days of Bacon's rebellion, having eaten some of this plant, which was boiled for salad by mistake, were made natural fools and buffoons by it for eleven days, without injury to their bodies (? ?). —May 29, 1851

In the excerpt above, Thoreau wrote about the jimsonweed, quoting from Jacob Bigelow's book, *American Medical Botany*. The question marks at the end are Thoreau's, and it should be noted that Thoreau was wrong to include the common name apple of Peru, which belongs to the cultivated plant *Nicandra physalodes*.

It is said that Linnaeus derived the name *Datura* from the words for "dare," and "to give," because the plants were given to those whose sexual powers had weakened. But *Webster's Second International Dictionary* indicates that the word is from the Hindu *dhatura*, the native word for the plant.

On the beach at Hull, and afterwards all along the shore to
Plymouth, I saw the datura, the variety (red-stemmed),
methinks, which some call Tatula *instead of* Stramonium
[for years the name of Datura Tatula *was applied to purple-*
flowered forms]. I felt as if I was on the highway of the
world, at sight of this cosmopolite and veteran traveler. It
told of commerce and sailors' yarns without end. It grows
luxuriantly in sand and gravel. This Captain Cook among
plants, this Norseman or sea pirate, Viking or king of the
bays, the beaches. It is not an innocent plant; it suggests
commerce, with its attendant vices. —*July 25, 1851*

Dioscorides, a first-century Greek physician, wrote in *The Greek Herbal of Dioscorides* that "the root being drunk with wine in the quantity of a dram, hath the power to effect not unpleasant phantasies. But two drams being drunk, make him beside himself for three days, and four being drunk kill him." In 1694, John Pechey wrote that "wenches give half a dram of it to their lovers, in beer or wine. Some are so skilled in the dosing of it, that they can make a man mad for as many hours as they please."

The hallucinatory stories continue in Robert Beverly's *History and Present State of Virginia,* from 1765. Beverly wrote that datura, "being an early plant, was gather'd very young for a boil'd salad, by some soldiers sent thither, to pacifie the troubles of Bacon; and some of them eat plentifully of it, the effect of which was a very unpleasant comedy; for they turn'd natural Fools upon it for Several Days: One would blow up a Feather in the Air; another would dart Straws at it with much Fury; and another stark naked was sitting up in a Corner, like a Monkey, grinning and making Mows at them; a Fourth would fondly kiss, and paw his Companions, and sneer in their faces, with a countenance more antick, than any in a Dutch Droll."

As a result of their behavior, the men were locked up, and eleven days passed before they snapped back to reality. The "troubles of Bacon" referred to Nathaniel Bacon's 1676 rebellion against the civil authorities to protest the failure of the Virginia governor to protect the colony from the Indians.

According to *John Banister and His Natural History of Virginia*, by Joseph and Nesta Ewan, *Datura stramonium* was perhaps introduced in 1614 as weed seed when *Nicotiana tabacum* was brought from Trinidad or even earlier as an Indian trade item for use in huskanaws or other ceremonies. (Huskanaws were tribal initiation rites for youths at puberty that included fasting and the use of narcotics.) Banister also describes the antics of Bacon's soldiers, who made a "boil'd Salad" from some young shoots of Jamestown weed and had to be confined "lest they should in their Folly destroy themselves; though it was observed, that all their Actions were full of Innocence and good Nature."

Neltje Blanchan writes that the Indians called datura the white man's plant and associated it with the Jamestown settlement. She asserts that Raleigh's colonists would have been more than likely to carry with them the seeds of this herb because it yielded an alkaloid more esteemed in the England of their day than the alkaloid of opium known as morphine. Gardeners of that time were said to banish it from their yards only because of the "rank odor of the leaves." But gardeners and anybody with a backyard should be advised that present-day references on medicinal plants point out that the whole plant contains atropine and other alkaloids used to dilate the pupils and, because they impede the action of the parasympathetic nervous system, to treat Parkinson's disease. Extracts of the plant have been used in behind-the-ear patches for treating vertigo, and the leaves were once smoked as an antispasmodic for asthma. But many fatalities from ingesting this plant have been recorded over the years, and people with sensitive skin must be careful never to put fingers that have touched the leaves anywhere near the eyes.

By 1859, Thoreau had found out something more about daturas.

You find henbane and Jamestown-weed and the like in cellars,
—such herbs as the witches are said to put into their caldron.
. . . It would fit that the tobacco plant should spring up on
the house-site, aye on the grave, of almost every house-
holder of Concord. These vile weeds are sown by vile men.
When the house is gone they spring up in the corners of cellars
where the cider-casks stood always on tap, for murder and all
kindred vices will out. And that rank crowd which lines the
gutter, where the wash of the dinner dishes flows, are but
more distant parasites of the host. What obscene and poisonous
weeds, think you, will mark the site of a Slave State?—what
kind of Jamestown-weed?   *—September 22, 1859*

While writing *The Evening Garden,* I ran across the story of
Jamestown soldiers brewing coffee from datura seeds, killing as
many as 166 men. Where did this story come from?

Perhaps the answer lies in an anecdote reported in *Wild Flowers
of the United States, The Southeastern States,* by Harold William
Rickett. Under the entry for datura, the story is told of "an old
Negro couple, too poor to buy coffee, who brewed the seeds of
Jimsonweed from their backyard, as a substitute. They were found
a day or two later, quite dead."

Thoughts of morbidity aside, the flowers are quite beautiful,
usually opening up around twilight when they are pollinated by
sphinx moths. On dark afternoons, they may open earlier and be
approached by flies, bees, and an occasional beetle.

In Thoreau's Garden datura would be planted in drifts, ready
to open its flowers to all the moths in the neighborhood. In the real
garden I keep the thorn apple about, although I'm now very careful where I plant it, as the following story shows.

Every year I let one plant of the jimsonweed grow at our front
stoop. Most of its foliage is hidden behind the luxurious leaves of
white four-o'clocks (*Mirabilis jalapa*), a vesper plant grown by
Thomas Jefferson but unmentioned by Thoreau. Last year the UPS

deliveryman, dressed in shorts, brushed against a few jimsonweed leaves that grew out and over the other plants. When he returned a few days later, I noticed a rash on his leg.

"It's contact dermatitis," he said. "I must have hit something that I'm allergic to."

"Poison ivy?"

"Could be, but I've never been bothered by it before."

I volunteered no other information but made sure that I moved the one specimen of jimsonweed a bit farther away.

THE HORSETAILS
Equisetum spp.

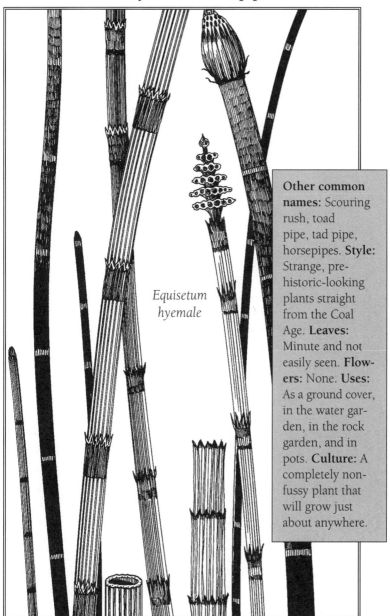

Equisetum hyemale

Other common names: Scouring rush, toad pipe, tad pipe, horsepipes. **Style:** Strange, pre-historic-looking plants straight from the Coal Age. **Leaves:** Minute and not easily seen. **Flowers:** None. **Uses:** As a ground cover, in the water garden, in the rock garden, and in pots. **Culture:** A completely non-fussy plant that will grow just about anywhere.

A strong and wholesome fragrance now from the vegetation as I go by overgrown paths through the swamp west of Nut Meadow. Equisetum hyemale has been out a good while; it is mostly effete, but some open yet. Some have flower spikes on the sides near the top, but most one at top, of the last year's plant. This year's shoots a foot high, more or less.

—May 12, 1860

Horsetails are represented by one genus, *Equisetum*. There are about twenty species found around the world except in Australia and New Zealand, with the most luxuriant types growing throughout the tropics. The scientific name comes from the Latin *equus*, horse, and *seta*, tail.

Thoreau recognized three species of horsetails; the field horsetail (*Equisetum arvense*), the scouring rush, or greater horsetail (*E. hyemale*), and a third species that lacks a specific common name, *E. fluviatile*, known as *E. limosum* in the mid-1800s.

What is that green pipe on the side-hill at Nut Meadow on his land, looking at first like green-briar cut off. It forms a dense bed about a dozen rods along the side of the bank in the woods, a rod in width, rising to ten or twelve feet above the swamp. White Pond mostly skimmed over. The scouring-rush is as large round as a bulrush, forming dense green beds conspicuous and interesting above the snow, an evergreen rush.

—December 6, 1854

When Thoreau wrote the above description he must have been looking at a cultivar of *Equisetum hyemale*. In the continental United States, the only horsetail of that height was named *Equisetum robustum* in 1844 but changed to 'Robustum' in 1903.

Thoreau continued to be attracted by horsetails, or horsepipes, as they were called back then. "Cloudy and rain, threatening withal," he wrote on the first of June in 1855. When surveying at Holden woodlot, he noticed the common scouring rush (*Equisetum hyemale*), and called attention to its black-scaled flowerets, often separated so as to show the green between, but not in open rings or whorls like *E. fluviatile*. He also measured the pipes of *E. fluviatile* and found they were generally three to seven inches high, but still so brown that he mistook them at a little distance for brown stubble amid the green of springing sedge, and not a fresh growth at all. And he mistakenly referred to flowerets; these plants do not flower but bear spores.

Equisetum hyemale is called the common scouring rush because its stems have such a high silica content that in pioneer days handfuls were used to scour cabin floors and clean cooking utensils. If you're ever caught without a Brillo pad on a camping trip, look for a bunch of these odd plants, and you won't have any excuse for dirty frying pans. The dry stems are useful for polishing both wood and metal. Because of the Dutch reputation for cleanliness, in Europe *Equisetum hyemale* is called the Dutch rush.

Here in North America the scouring rush grows along streams, lakes, swamps, in roadside ditches, and often on the edges of old railroad beds. Over the years, such thickets have appeared because railroad cooks threw out used wads of horsetails, left from cleaning up the dishes.

The evergreen shoots grow from a perennial rhizome (or thickened root). Because they are not fussy about drainage, I keep a large clump in a nine-inch pot without a drainage hole. All summer the pot sits in the full sun and is brought inside in early fall to the sun porch. An eight-inch pot holds a clump set out in the middle of a small pool, and when a dragonfly alights, it looks like a small throwback to prehistoric times.

Horsetails arose millions of years ago and flourished from the late Devonian to the Triassic, when the average stem was over thirty-six feet high with a ten-inch diameter. Dragonflies with fourteen-inch wingspans flitted about the hot, musty swamps amid ferns that also topped thirty feet, all under a burning tropical sun in an atmosphere of volcanic clouds. These gigantic horsetails served as walkways for giant cockroaches and spiders.

When these mounds of vegetation died, they sank deep into the waters of their swampland home. Millions of years passed and chemical action eventually turned the plants into one of the main constituents of coal.

Although horsetails seem to appreciate acid soil, they are also found growing on gravel bars and in sand dunes. These last habitats point out their potential use in xerotropic gardening. *Equisetum* probably tolerates xeric conditions because of its very small leaves with their smaller breathing pores (or stomata) and because the plant's rhizome will penetrate deep into the soil, often over six feet.

Tiny, scalelike, pennant-shaped leaves encircle the rings that connect the hollow stems, where the major portion of photosynthesis occurs. Individual stem sections can be pulled apart like pop-it beads and temporarily stuck back together.

Horsetails are too primitive to produce seeds. Instead, like ferns, they produce spores that fall from the terminal conelike spikes found on many branches. Spores germinate on the surface of the ground and grow into gamete-producing prothallia. An individual prothallus is about a sixteenth of an inch across and resembles a tiny bright green leaf. Prothallia contain special cells called antheridia, which produce sperm, and archegonia, which produce eggs.

Following fertilization, a zygote divides into four cells. The top two cells become the stem and the first leaves, and the bottom two become the root.

The whole plant has been used in folk remedies. The American Indians made tea from the stems for the treatment of kidney and bladder ailments, and roots were often given to teething babies. Today's medical authorities caution against any medicinal use of the plant, especially since ingestion of its compounds disturbs thiamine metabolism. Years ago, horses often died after grazing on horsetails in early spring, while waiting for meadow grasses to green up.

Plants left outside usually receive enough moisture from rainwater. I will water them during a dry summer, however. For potting soil use two parts standard mix to one part coarse sand or gravel. If the clumps begin to crack the pot, it's time to divide the clump.

The conelike caps look like the miniaturized domes of a Far Eastern church. The whorls of tiny, scalelike leaves that circle the stems every few inches give the plant a strange beauty. Add to this the strong, upright stems—especially those of the cultivar 'Robustum'—and you have a truly exotic addition to any wild, or civilized, garden.

Among the species available today, look for *Equisetum diffusum,* a tropical horsetail with small, soft, gray-green stems that form little thickets; it's a perfect houseplant.

Though many Japanese flower arrangers think that *Equisetum hyemale* 'Robustum' is a new cultivar, it was first recognized in 1844. Like all the others, it can be confined to the proper area by using a plastic or metal band or ring.

Equisetum variegatum has stems up to two feet tall circled with greenish yellow rings below a ring of black leaves. This species does better than the others in light to medium shade.

Equisetum scirpoides, the dwarf scouring rush, forms a tangled mat of tiny wiry stalks and is perfect in the rock garden—but be careful because it, too, spreads.

DOG-DAY FLOWERS

You now see and hear no red-wings, along the river as in spring. See the blue herons opposite Fair Haven Hill, as if they had bred there. This and the last day or two very hot. Now at last, *methinks, the most melting season of the year, though I think it is hardly last year's bathing time, because the water is higher. There is very little air over the water, and when I dip my head in for coolness, I do not feel any coldness. The* Eupatorium sessilifolium *has been out a day or two on the side-hill grove at Bittern Cliff [across the river from Fair Haven Hill]; very similar its leaves and form to the small sunflower.* Desmodium Canadense *(?), apparently a good while; perhaps with the earliest. Never saw it before. Has dense racemes of large flowers and pods. In the same place. I find, on the Cliff there, a* Gerardia quercifolia *which answers to the book (Gray)* [Gray's Manual of Botany], *though I have not perhaps the* lowest leaves. *It has the linear-lanceolate segments of calyx. My last had not, though it was glaucous and was much more cut-leaved. There are varieties of the glaucous, then. They are both less densely spiked than the flava. Panicled cornel berries begin. The river cornel berries just beginning in this sunny place.* Chelone glabra *also. The round-leaved desmodium, a good while, and still on the hillside beyond the elm; perhaps ten days. Was that a thistle-down over the river, without the seed? Carried watermelons for drink. What more refreshing and convenient! This richest wine in a convenient cask, and so easily kept cool! No foreign wines could be so grateful. The first muskmelon to-day. If you would cool a watermelon, do not put it in water, which keeps the heat in, but cut it open and set it in a cellar or in the shade, or in a draught. If you have carriage, carry these green bottles of wine. A good many lilies yet rested in the shade under the bridges.* —August 11, 1853

The Conantum Cliff looks out over the Sudbury River, and Thoreau once thought of buying it but for want of money could not come to terms. On the day described above, he left his house at 9:00 A.M. and went to Conantum by boat to gather berries. He was accompanied by three ladies. On August 12, the boat continued, but without the ladies.

The last was a melting night, and a carnival for mosquitoes. Could I not write meditations under a bridge at midsummer? The last three or four days less dogdayish. We paused under each bridge yesterday,—we who had been sweltering on the quiet waves,—for the sake of a little shade and coolness, holding on by the piers with our hands. Now and then a muskrat made the water boil, which dove or came up near by. They will move so suddenly in the water when alarmed as to make quite a report.

Hibiscus just beginning to open, its large cylindrical buds, as long as your finger, fast unrolling. They look like loosely rolled pink cigars. Rowed home in haste before a black approaching storm from the northeast, which was slightly cooling the air. How grateful when, as I backed through the bridges, the breeze of the storm blew through the piers, rippling the water and slightly cooling the sultry air! How fast the black cloud came up, and passed over my head, proving all wind!   —*August 12, 1853*

The Time-Honored Joe-Pye Weeds
Eupatorium spp.

Style: A tall, stately plant with fluffy purple flowers beloved by swallowtail butterflies. **Leaves:** Three to eight inches long in whorls of three to five. **Flowers:** Individual flowers a third of an inch wide, in clusters up to six inches long. **Uses:** In the water garden, the wild garden, and the perennial border. **Culture:** Good, evenly moist soil, in full sun.

Eupatorium purpureum

Brought home a great Eupatorium purpureum *from Miles's Swamp. It is ten and a half feet high and one inch in diameter; said to grow to twelve feet. The corymb, eighteen and a half inches wide by fifteen inches deep; the largest leaves, thirteen by three inches. The stem hollow throughout. This, I found, to my surprise, when I undertook to make a flute of it, trusting it was closed at the leaves; but there is no more pith there than elsewhere. It would serve many purposes, as a water-pipe, etc. Probably the Indians knew and used it. They might have blowed arrows through a straight one. It would yield an available hollow tube six feet long.* —August 20, 1854

To dig up an entire joe-pye would be a great job even out of season and using earth-moving equipment, so I knew when Thoreau wrote the above, he was describing only one stem and not the whole plant.

Joe-pye will tower above everything else in its neighborhood except a nearby tree, but trees are not usually found growing in ditches or at the end of low-lying meadows where this plant does its best. Don't let the size of the plant deter you; even the smallest garden must have spot for this stately wildflower.

The pale, dull magenta or sometimes lavender pink flowers form compound clusters on top of strong, straight stems. They have a faint fragrance that acts as a magnet to butterflies in the area. I've counted ten yellow swallowtails on one blossom that was moving back and forth in a stiff summer breeze, never breaking the plant's stem nor bothering the butterflies, either.

A Caucasian of old New England who palmed himself off as an American Indian medicine man, Joe-Pye was famed among his white neighbors for his skill in curing the devastating typhoid fever that, along with the so-called hereditary consumption, was exterminating a number of New England families. His cure-all was a bitter tea concocted from the leaves and stalks of *Eupatorium purpureum*. In token of his unproved success the plant bears his name, but it is now wholly neglected by the herb doctor.

According to contemporary authorities, Joe used the plant to induce sweating, thus adding to the cure. American Indians also used the plant as a medicine. The entire herb was employed as a diuretic for dropsy, painful urination, colds, chills, fevers, and even rheumatism.

A few cultivars have turned up on the garden market, including *Eupatorium purpureum* 'Atropurpureum', a plant that grows to seven feet rather than the typical twelve and has flowers that are a darker shade of rose purple. With flowering heads often eighteen inches across, the plant is a truly fine addition to the back of the border or the wild garden, or it can be used as a specimen plant, where a healthy clump can almost assume the proportions of a small tree.

The three species usually found are *Eupatorium purpureum,* *E. maculatum,* a shorter plant with purple-spotted stems, and *E. fistulosum.* This third species has given rise to the white-flowered cultivar 'Album', and has been given the somewhat fanciful name of "Joe Pye's Bride" by Alan Bush of Holbrook Farm. At a bit over four feet, this new introduction promises to be the best species for very small gardens. These plants are hardy to USDA Zone 4 and do especially well in ground that is continually damp—even wet. Under these conditions the magnificent flowers really take off.

Even at summer's end when the frost comes and winter is in the wings, the browned flower heads of the joe-pye are still attractive. At the end of September in 1851, Thoreau noted that "the *Eupatorium purpureum* is early killed by frost and stands now all dry and brown by the sides of other herbs like goldenrod and tansy, which are quite green and in blossom."

Just after Christmas in 1855, he wrote, "[Now is] a good time to walk in swamps, there being ice but no snow to speak of,—all crust. It is a good walk along the edge of the river, the wild side, amid the button-bushes and willows. The eupatorium stalks still stand there, with their brown hemispheres of little twigs, orreries."

The Rose Hibiscus
Hibiscus palustris

Style: Big, blousy tropical-looking flowers on tall stems, often seven feet. **Leaves:** Three to seven inches long, tapering and pointed. **Flowers:** Four to seven inches across, a clear rose pink, sometimes white, often with a crimson center. **Zone:** 6. **Uses:** In both the civilized and the wild garden, especially in wet places. **Culture:** Full sun in damp, but not rich, soil. Needs watering in dry summers.

> Hibiscus moscheutos, *marsh hibiscus . . . perchance has*
> *been out a week. I think it must be the most conspicuous*
> *and showy and at the same time rich-colored flower of this*
> *month. It is not so conspicuous as the sunflower, but of a*
> *rarer color,—"pale rose-purple," they call it,—like a holly-*
> *hock. It is surprising for its amount of color, and, seen un-*
> *expectedly amid the willows and button-bushes, with the*
> *mikania twining around its stem, you can hardly believe it is*
> *a flower, so large and tender it looks, like the greatest effort*
> *of the season to adorn the August days, and reminded me of*
> *that great tender moth, the* Actias luna, *which I found on*
> *the water near where it grows.*   —*August 16, 1852*

THE ROSE MALLOW, OR MARSH HIBISCUS, IS FOUND IN MARSHES ALONG THE
coast and inland to Maryland, southern Ohio, and Indiana, then
south to the Gulf of Mexico. If Thoreau had lived a bit farther west,
he would probably have missed this most beautiful of wildflowers.
In Thoreau's time the plant was called *Hibiscus moscheutos*, but the
name has been changed to *H. palustris.*

Every night in Thoreau's Garden these tropical blossoms
would attract not one but a score of luna moths that would flutter
around the exotic petals, keeping their wings open slightly past
dawn so that their chartreuse color would be seen to complement
the pink of the rose mallows.

The milkania that Thoreau mentions was once called *Willug-*
baeya scandens in honor of Francis Willughby (1635–1671), an
English naturalist. This vine has been renamed *Mikania scandens* to
commemorate an eighteenth-century professor, J. G. Mikan, and
his son, J. C. Mikan, who collected plants in Brazil. It is also known
as the climbing hempvine.

> *The hibiscus flowers are seen a quarter of a mile off over the*
> *water, like large roses, now that these high colors are rather*
> *rare. Some are exceedingly delicate and pale, almost white,*

just rose-tinted, others a brighter pink or rose-color, and all slightly plaited (the five large petals) and turned toward the sun, now in the west, trembling in the wind. So much color looks very rich in these localities. . . . A superb flower.

—August 18, 1852

These wild hibiscus are so impressive that today's *Hibiscus palustris* has been crossed with tropical species to produce the summer annuals and perennials that sport giant blossoms as bright as Brazilian sunsets and as big across as dessert plates. According to many authorities, these plants are not affected by salt, and suggestions have been made to plant them where winter highway runoff has salted the earth, making it poisonous to many of our wild plants.

The Desmodium Path

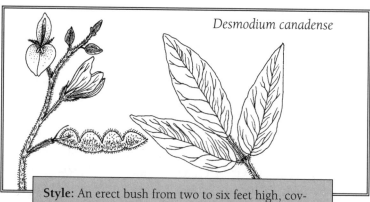

Desmodium canadense

Style: An erect bush from two to six feet high, covered with terminal clusters of pink or rose-purple pealike flowers. **Leaves:** Compounded of three oblong leaflets, the center the largest. **Flowers:** Butterfly shaped and about a half inch long. **Fruit:** A hairy segmented pod about an inch long and covered with tiny bristles. **Uses:** Only in the wild garden. **Culture:** Reasonably good soil in full sun.

*Lespedezas and desmodiums are now generally in prime.
The latter are an especially interesting family, with commonly such delicate, spreading panicles, the plants themselves in their distribution so scattered and inobvious, and
the open and spreading panicle of commonly verdigris-
green flowers (in drying) make them to be unobserved when
you are near them. The panicle of flowers often as large
or larger than all the rest of the plant, with their peculiar
chain-like seedpods, rhomboidal or semiorbicular, or with
concave backs. They love dry hillsides. They are not so
abundant, after all, but I feel an agreeable surprise as often
as I come across a new locality for desmodiums. Rarely find
one kind without one or two more species near, their great
spreading panicles, yet delicate, open, and airy, occupying
the August air.*   —*August 19, 1856*

DESMODIUMS AREN'T CALLED TICK-TREFOILS FOR NOTHING. TREFOIL
refers to the three leaves, and *tick* refers to the ability of the segmented pods to break up into individual, one-seeded fragments
that stick like ticks to clothing when one walks through the fields
of autumn.

*I go along plum path behind Adolphus Clark's. This is a pe-
culiar locality for plants. The Desmodium Canadense is
now apparently in its prime there and very common, with
its rather rich spikes of purple flowers, —the most (?) conspicuous of the desmodiums. It might be called Desmodium
Path. Also the small rough sunflower (now abundant) and
the common apocynum (also in bloom as well as going and
gone to seed) are very common.*   —*August 11, 1858*

And Thoreau plus every other creature walking the Desmodium Path would take along a seed or two of tick-trefoil to a new
destination and a new place for a plant to grow.

The False Foxgloves
Gerardia spp.

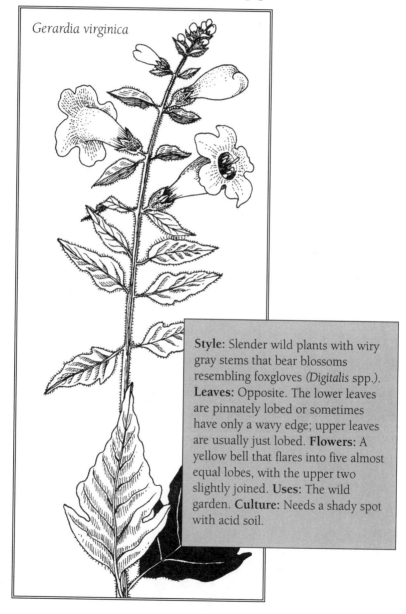

Gerardia virginica

Style: Slender wild plants with wiry gray stems that bear blossoms resembling foxgloves *(Digitalis* spp.). **Leaves:** Opposite. The lower leaves are pinnately lobed or sometimes have only a wavy edge; upper leaves are usually just lobed. **Flowers:** A yellow bell that flares into five almost equal lobes, with the upper two slightly joined. **Uses:** The wild garden. **Culture:** Needs a shady spot with acid soil.

[I will] sail and paddle to find a place where the bank has a more neglected look. I wish to bury myself amid reeds. I pine for the luxuriant vegetation of the river-banks.
I ramble over the wooded hill on the right beyond the Pantry. The bushy gerardia is now very conspicuous with its great yellow trumpets, on hillsides on sprout-lands. Sometimes you come upon a large field of them. The buds or closed tubes are as handsome, at least, as the flowers.

—*August 31, 1852*

FORTUNATELY, THE GERARDIAS, OR FALSE FOXGLOVES, ARE SUCH BEAUTIFUL flowers that in spite of their cultural demands, their part in our imaginary Thoreau's Garden makes it worthwhile to sort out the nomenclatural changes from Thoreau's day to ours.

The four plants usually seen in the woods and along mountain trails are the downy false foxglove *(Gerardia virginica)*, the smooth false foxglove *(G. laevigata)*, the yellow false foxglove *(G. flava)*, and the fern-leaved false foxglove *(G. pedicularia)*. They take their names from the herbalist John Gerarde. They are usually listed as being uncultivable because they are partially parasitic on the roots of oaks.

Gerardia is the genus name bestowed by Asa Gray in *Gray's Manual of Botany* (New York: American Book Company, 1895), and that book's scientific names were used in *A Field Guide to Wildflowers of Northeastern and North-central North America,* by Roger Tory Peterson and Margaret McKenny (Boston: Houghton Mifflin Company, 1968). However, Peterson's identifications do not match those of most other botanical books.

For example, *Wild Flowers of the United States* (New York Botanical Garden, New York: McGraw-Hill Book Company, 1966) trades *Gerardia* for *Aureolaria* (from the Latin *aureolus,* or golden), and so do *The New Britton and Brown Illustrated Flora of the Northeastern United States and Adjacent Canada* (New York Botanical Garden, New York: Hafner Publishing Company, 1963) and *Hortus Third* (New York: Macmillan Publishing Company, 1976).

> *In the open oak wood beneath the Cliff, in the steep path and*
> *by its side, [are] the* Gerardia quercifolia *and also* flava. *The*
> *former is glaucous and all the leaves much cut, rather pinnate,*
> *as I remember, somewhat like Roman wormwood, but the*
> *calyx-lobes triangular and not more than a third or a fourth the*
> *length of the calyx-tube. It differs from Gray's G.* quercifolia
> *in the calyx-lobes not being long and linear. I will put it with*
> G. flava. *These are both among the most remarkable flowers*
> *at present, so large and butter-yellow. Very rich they look, with*
> *their great trumpets. A bee has eaten a round hole in the side*
> *of an unopened flower. How few flowers and fruits blossom*
> *and ripen without being deformed by worms and insects!*
> *You must search for perfect specimens.* —*August 8, 1853*

Thoreau's flowers match *Dasystoma virginica* (also listed as
Gerardia quercifolia) pictured in Britton and Brown's *An Illustrated
Flora of the Northern United States, Canada and the British Possessions*
(New York: Charles Scribner's Sons, 1896). Its common name is
the smooth false foxglove, and the leaf outline looks exactly like an
oak leaf (*quercus*, oak, plus *folia*, leaves). Hence this plant, Thoreau's
Gerardia quercifolia, and *Aureolaria virginica* are all the same.
(*Dasystoma* is Greek for "thick or hairy mouth," referring to the
five-lobed corolla, or floral lip.) Thoreau confused this plant with
G. flava because the flowers are almost identical.

> *On the west side of Emerson's Cliff, I notice many* Gerardia
> pedicularia *out. A bee is hovering about one bush. The*
> *flowers are not yet open, and if they were, perhaps he would*
> *not enter. He proceeds at once, head downward to the base*
> *of the tube, extracts the sweet there, and departs.*
> *Examining, I find that every flower has a small hole*
> *pierced through the tube, commonly through calyx and all,*
> *opposite the nectary. This does not hinder its opening. The*
> *Rape of the Flower! The bee knew where the sweet lay, and*

was unscrupulous in his mode of obtaining it. A certain vio-
lence tolerated by nature.   —*August 22, 1856*

The bee-plundered flower is the fern-leafed gerardia, or the lousewort false foxglove (*Aureolaria pedicularia*). The common name refers to this gerardia's passing resemblance to a lousewort (probably the wood-betony, or *Pedicularis lanceolata*).

Contemporary books list this false foxglove as an annual. That means that if seed could be gathered then planted at the base of or in the vicinity of an oak tree, this particular plant could be garden grown. I'm beginning my search for seed today!

The Turtleheads
Chelone spp.

Style: Snapdragons on two-foot stalks, reveling in wet soil. **Leaves:** Opposite, ovate leaves to six inches long. **Flowers:** Look like a turtle's head. **Uses:** Excellent for the edge of the water garden, along streams, and in the perennial border if given enough water. **Culture:** Needs soil rich in humus and nearly full sun.

Chelone glabra

. . . chelone six feet high! —*August 16, 1856*

MOST COMMON NAMES FOR WILDFLOWERS ARE EITHER QUITE LITERAL, very imaginative, or both; turtleheads qualify as both. When viewed from the side, these strange but beautiful white blossoms look like the heads of lizards or turtles. The scientific name is *Chelone glabra*. *Chelone* is Greek for tortoise and *glabra* means that the flower lacks hairs. They bloom in late summer and on into fall.

Turtleheads are more than happy in wet soil, especially at the edges of creeks and rills, but will also do well in moist garden soil. This is especially true if you use plenty of humus when planting and make sure to add water during periods of dry weather. If cultural conditions are to the plant's liking, it will easily reach a height of three feet. The stems are strong and will not need staking. Bebe Miles once told me to nip off the tender tips when spring plants reach a height of about six inches. This produces bushy and branching plants, slightly shorter but with more flowers.

According to Neltje Blanchan in her wonderful book *Nature's Garden,* "It requires something of a struggle for even so strong and vigorous an insect as the bumblebee to gain admission to the inhospitable-looking flower before maturity."

When young, the upper part and the lower part of the tubed flower are almost sealed, but when mature, the bee's weight plus energetic prying with its head allows the insect to get inside to the nectar and leave with attached pollen. But for a few moments, it looks like the flower is eating the bee. Unfortunately, deer like the flowers, too.

The natural range of the plant is from Newfoundland to Ontario and Minnesota and south to Georgia, Alabama, and Missouri. *Chelone lyonii* is a pink-flowered species from the southern mountains that is hardy up north if given a damp site. It blooms later than the white-flowered *glabra*. From southern swamps, *Chelone obliqua* has almost purple flowers and is hardy to the north of Philadelphia. Propagation is by division in the spring and by seed.

DYER'S GREENWEED
Genista tinctoria

Style: A low, branching shrub from one to two feet high, the stems and branches erect and nearly or quite smooth. **Leaves:** Light green, one to one and a half inches long, lance shaped. **Flowers:** Resembling bean blossoms, the bright yellow flowers hang in slender terminal clusters from one to two inches long. **Fruit:** The several-seeded pods are flat and about an inch long. **Uses:** Colorful additions to the flower border, especially because they bloom when most of spring's flowers are finished. After blooming, they become a backdrop to flowering summer annuals. **Culture:** Full sunshine, a light, sandy soil with good drainage. Moved with difficulty.

*The Genista tinctoria has been open apparently a week. It
has a pretty and lively effect, reminding me for some reason
of the poverty grass.* —June 28, 1858.

Five weeks after that day in June, Thoreau wrote about a walk to
Boulder Field, a place just off the Old Carlisle Road that met
Lowell Road at Hunt's Bridge.

*The broom is quite out of bloom, probably a week or ten
days. It is almost ripe, indeed. I should like to see how
rapidly it spreads. The dense roundish masses, side by side,
are three or four feet over and fifteen inches high. They have
grown from near the ground this year. The whole clump is
now about eighteen feet from north to south by twelve wide.
Within a foot or two of its edge, I detect many slender little
plants springing up in the grass, only three inches high, but,
on digging, am surprised to find that they are two years old.
They have large roots, running down straight as well as
branching, much stouter than the part above ground. Thus
it appears to spread slowly by the seed falling from its edge,
for I detected no runners.* —August 6, 1858

Dyer's greenweed, or broom, is a slender shrub up to forty
inches tall, with simple leaves and bright yellow pealike flowers
followed by inch-long flat little pods that contain just a few seeds
each. A native of Europe, it's found on heaths, in grassy places, and
in scree, and its range extends to Asia Minor and the Ukraine; ab-
sent from most of the islands of the Mediterranean, it's also found
in Sicily. Brought to America, it escaped from cultivation sometime
during the late 1700s, and by the early 1900s had made its way
from Maine to Massachusetts and to eastern New York, where it
preferred dry hilltops and sterile soil. By the middle of the century,
this small shrub with its sparkling yellow flowers had reached
western New York and wandered down to Virginia.

Containing luteolin, a yellow glycoside dye, dyer's greenweed has been known since Roman times as a coloring agent, used especially for dying wool either yellow or green. Once used as a diuretic and laxative, the seeds contain two alkaloids, cytisine and methyl-cytisine.

William Robinson, the English gardener who attacked the formal restraints of Victorian culture and high Victorian gardens in his book *The Wild Garden,* wrote about genista, claiming that in the pea family "there are a few plants of great merit, and the first we meet is the very pretty dwarf shrub *Genista tinctoria,* or Dyer's genista. This is a little shrub, but vigorous in the profusion of its yellow flowers, and would be at home on any rough banks or grassy places, or among dwarf shrubs. It is frequent in England, but rare in Scotland and Ireland."

You can tell just how popular a plant is by the number of common names to its credit, and all the following refer to this particular genista: alleluia, brummel, greening-weed, sarrat, shebroom, waxen wood, woadmesh, woadwax, woadwise, woodas, woodwax, and woodwaxen. The use of the word *woad* salutes the English woad *(Isatis tinctoria),* a plant whose leaves yield a blue dye. According to Caesar, British fighting men painted themselves with woad, and Pliny claimed that British women stained their bodies with woad and walked naked in various religious ceremonies.

In *Field Book of American Trees and Shrubs,* F. Schuyler Mathews quotes from an undated letter from Charles Arthur King of Plainfield, New Jersey: "It grows in greatest profusion on Cape Cod, and is a conspicuous bright and beautiful member of the varied flora of the moorlands." Schuyler refers to genista as "whin," an old Welsh word for gorse or furze *(Ulex europaeus),* a member of the family that covers many of the hills of England, extending onto the tablelands of Dartmoor (wrote Robert Burns, "Through the whins, and by the cairn").

According to most dye manuals, genista was used to give a yellow as a basis for green, by dyeing the material first with woodwax, then with woad. Or blue wool was greened up with genista, hence the term greening-weed. The combination produced the celebrated Kendal green, named for the city Kendal in the county Westmorland, where the process was used by Flemish immigrants during the reign of Edward III. The plant was thought valuable enough for New World settlers to take it along to New England. In 1672, John Josselyn wrote about it in his book *New-England's Rarities:* "woodwax, wherewith they dye many pretty Colours."

It's easily missed when not in bloom, and according to Geoffrey Grigson in *The Englishman's Flora,* it "often grows with a cheerful, tough persistence in the tangle of old grass along roads and lanes; or sometimes, as you go by in the train, you glimpse a colony in possession of a railway embankment."

During the late nineteenth century, a double-flowered form known as 'Plena' was grown as a pot plant and called by Samuel Wood in his *A Plain Guide to Good Gardening* (1891) "a remarkably pretty dwarf free-flowering plant." But according to Krussman in his *Manual of Cultivated Broad-leaved Trees and Shrubs,* 'Plena' was around before 1835. Because of its procumbent form, 'Plena' is especially attractive in the rock garden. I've looked for this cultivar for years and only recently found a source not only for 'Plena' but also for 'Royal Gold', a form with larger and brighter flowers.

The new Royal Horticultural Society's *Dictionary of Gardening* mentions the cultivar 'Golden Plate', with spreading habit, weeping branches, and flowers of clear yellow.

Other varieties include *hirsuta,* more strongly branched than the species, having lightly pubescent young branches and leaves, and *humilior,* another procumbent form that usually flowers earlier in the season.

> *The pods of the broom are nearly half of them open. I perceive that one, just ready to open, opens with a slight spring on being touched, and the pods at once twist and curl a little.*

I suspect that such seeds as these, which the winds do not transport, will turn out to be more sought after by birds, etc., and so transported by them than those lighter ones which are furnished with a pappus and are accordingly transported by the wind. —September 18, 1860

THE WILD GERANIUMS
Geranium spp.

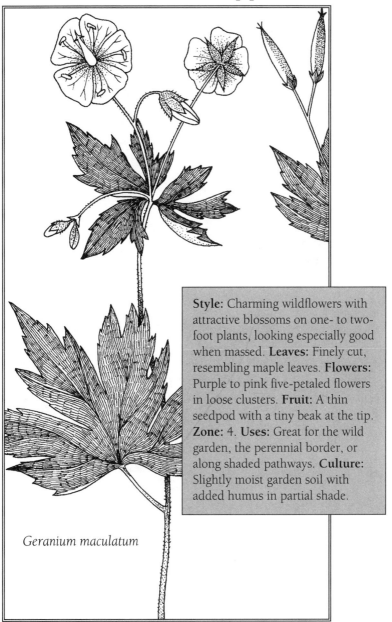

Geranium maculatum

Style: Charming wildflowers with attractive blossoms on one- to two-foot plants, looking especially good when massed. **Leaves:** Finely cut, resembling maple leaves. **Flowers:** Purple to pink five-petaled flowers in loose clusters. **Fruit:** A thin seedpod with a tiny beak at the tip. **Zone:** 4. **Uses:** Great for the wild garden, the perennial border, or along shaded pathways. **Culture:** Slightly moist garden soil with added humus in partial shade.

The geranium is a delicate flower and belongs especially to shady places under trees and shrubs,—better if about springs—in by-nooks, so modest.   *—May 30, 1852*

How beautiful the geranium flower-buds just opening!—little purple cylindrical tubes or hoods—cigaritos—with the petals lapped over and round each other. One opens visibly in a pitcher before me.   *—May 26, 1853*

The wild geraniums are not those blousy flowers of hot red, magenta, orange, or white that are planted in pots and boxes across bridges in American small towns or to decorate cemetery plots. Those popular plants are pelargoniums, originally from South Africa and brought to England and America by sailors. No, the true geraniums are hardy plants best suited for the perennial border or the wild garden. Derived from the Greek *geranos,* or crane, the botanical name refers to the similarity of the beaked seedpod to a crane's bill.

The best known of the wild geraniums is the wood geranium, or spotted cranesbill *(Geranium maculatum),* a perennial denizen of the woodland distributed from Maine to South Carolina and west to Canada, South Dakota, Kansas, and Arkansas.

A number of hardy geraniums from Europe are used today in the garden, many originally being popular plants in England. Most nursery catalogs list a number of species and cultivars. But for naturalizing or the wild garden, nothing beats the American native *Geranium maculatum,* with its loose clusters of pink to lavender purple, five-petaled flowers sitting atop one- to two-foot stalks adorned with finely cut leaves.

Thoreau knew this flower well. On one of his nature walks he saw buttercups and geraniums covering the meadows, the geraniums appearing to float on the grass. "Some geraniums are rose-colored, other pale purplish-blue, others whitish."

When not in flower the plants are still an attractive addition to the garden because of their leaves, usually described by botanical books as palmately cleft into five or seven lobes. Throughout the summer and into the fall, a few wood geranium leaves will suddenly turn red, acting like flaming beacons in a world of green.

> *I see a geranium leaf turned red, in the shade of a copse; the same color with the woodbine seen yesterday. These leaves interest me as much as the flowers. I should like to have a complete list of those that are the first to turn red or yellow. How attractive is color, especially red; kindred this with the color of fruits in the harvest and skies in the evening.*
> *—July 30, 1852*

Where winters are not too frigid, the basal leaves are nearly evergreen. The plant grows from a tough rootstock, so set individuals about one foot apart and, once planted, let them be. If plants must be divided, be sure each piece of root has several eyes. By mulching the soil around the geraniums and keeping it weed-free, they will be encouraged to grow and eventually form a large clump of specimen plants.

As beautiful as the wood geranium is, my heart really belongs to herb Robert, a weedy geranium of North America, Eurasia, and North Africa. Thoreau mentions it only once—when he paused to rest in the wooded shade by a rocky rill and saw it growing in the company of foamflowers. There he not only saw the leaves of the *Geranium robertianum,* brushed with their "radical reddish tinge," but could smell their peculiar scent.

The plant has been in America for centuries and is often assumed to be a native plant, but it's an alien introduction. According to *Wild Flowers of the United States* (New York: McGraw-Hill Book Company, 1966), the flower is now found growing wild in rocky woods and banks from Newfoundland to Manitoba and southward to Maryland, West Virginia, Indiana, and Nebraska.

Depending on where it grows, herb Robert is described as an annual or a biennial, but it will usually flower the first year from seed. It's a plant of damp, poor, and shady soil and it will soon spread to the cracks in stone walls. The plants are covered with small pinkish violet blooms from early summer until frost. When the green stems mature, they turn red, and eventually the leaves are stained with crimson. The various rock garden societies occasionally offer a white form, 'Album'.

Never topping ten inches, herb Robert is an attractive ground cover and edging plant that, once established, will continue to self-seed. In fact, when ripe, the little seed containers go off like popguns, and the seeds fly!

In England the plant has more than eighty common names, ranging from bloody Mary and granny-thread-the-needle to dog's-toe and stinker bobs, not to mention the ominous death-come-quickly. Why so many names? Apparently because the plant has been connected with the supernatural and various folk heroes and goblins.

Writing in *Nature's Garden,* Neltje Blanchan supposes that the Robert for whom this "holy herb" was named was either St. Robert, a Benedictine monk, or Robert Duke of Normandy. But other authorities, who deal more with the darker part of humanity, ascribe the plant to Robin Goodfellow, who, if not treated well and fed with cream, was said to be vindictive and lose his temper, and to Knecht Ruprecht, who dressed in red at Christmas and hit children who were not well behaved.

In folk medicine a leaf tea of herb Robert was used to treat malaria, jaundice, and tuberculosis. A wash was also prepared in folk medicine to relieve the pain of swollen breasts and as a remedy for fistulas and ulcers.

Many authorities claim that the plant has a fetid odor when touched, a fact that might have something to do with common names like smell-up and stinking jenny. I wouldn't suggest rolling around in a patch, but you will probably never be bothered by any smell. I've often wondered how anybody living in medieval Europe could notice the odor of this or other plants, given all the competing smells of everyday life.

THE QUAKER LADIES, OR BLUETS
Houstonia spp.

Style: Lovely little flowers that appear in such profusion they actually carpet the ground, blooming in midspring. **Leaves:** The oblong basal leaves are about a half inch long; the stem leaves are opposite and very tiny. **Flowers:** About a half inch wide, usually of pale blue (sometimes almost white and sometimes very dark blue) with golden centers; the corolla is tubular with four flattish lobes. **Zone:** 5. **Uses:** Great wild perennials for the wild or meadow garden with some doing well in the rock garden. **Culture:** Full sun in the North with some shade in the South; well-drained, but moist, acid soil.

Houstonia caerulea

[The bluets] are most interesting now, before many other flowers are out, the grass high, and they have lost their freshness. I sit down by one dense bed of them to examine them. It's about three feet long and two or more wide. The flowers not only crowd one another, but are in several tiers, one above another, and completely hide the ground,—a mass of white. Counting those in a small place, I find that there are about three thousand flowers in a square foot. They are all turned a little toward the sun, and emit a refreshing odor. —May 5, 1860

On that beautiful day in spring Thoreau described the dense beds of *Houstonia* in the yard of the old Conantum house. To his eye some of the flowers showed a distinctly bluer shade when they were viewed from some distance.

Before I begin to rhapsodize about bluets, I have to confront the botanical name. *Hortus Third*, dated 1978, lists the genus as *Hedyotis;* the *Audubon Society Field Guide to North American Wildflowers* includes all the bluet species in the genus *Houstonia*, as do both the old and the new editions of Britton and Brown's flora, dated 1898 and 1952, respectively, as well as Rickett's *Wild Flowers of the United States,* published in 1966. Claude A. Barr, writing in *Jewels of the Plains,* calls the plant *Houstonia,* and he was a very careful and knowledgeable man. And both *Newcomb's Wildflower Guide* from 1977 and *Guide to the Vascular Plants of the Blue Ridge* from 1989 call them the same. So until corrected, I'll call them *Houstonia,* too. Neltje Blanchan reports that Linnaeus named the flower for Dr. William Houston, a young English physician, botanist, and collector, who died in South America in 1733, after an exhausting tramp about the Gulf of Mexico. The species name *caerulea* is another spelling of cerulean, the color of the sky after the passing of a Canadian high when the air is pure and clean. Unfortunately, in *The Plant Hunters* (New York: McGraw-Hill Book

Company, 1969), Alice M. Coats writes that Houston had nothing to do with the bluet, but she doesn't mention the true discoverer.

Harold Rickett writes that "when all species, all over the world, of *Houstonia* and *Hedyotis* are considered, it is impossible to separate the two genera." So for all practical purposes, houstonias are wildflowers of the temperate world and hedyotis, the tropical. I've looked for the meaning of *Hedyotis* in every reference at hand, but to no avail. *Hedy,* however, is a Greek word for sweet. The word *charming* seems to fit these blossoms like no other. Bluet is the most popular of the common names. Others include innocence, Quaker ladies, Quaker bonnets, and Venus's pride, all pointing to the beauty of these very small blossoms. The bluets' natural range is from Novia Scotia to Ontario and on to Wisconsin, then south to Georgia, Alabama, and Missouri.

Strangely, the bluets belong to the Rubiaceae, or the madder family, a collection of mostly tropical plants that includes coffee, quinine, gardenias, and two lonely species of the partridge berry, *Mitchella repens,* from American woods, and *M. undulata,* from the woods of Japan.

Thoreau spots a lumbering bumblebee that he calls a humble-bee preparing to insert its tongue in these tiny flowers. "It's a rather ludicrous sight. Of course they will not support him, except a little where they are densest; so he bends them down rapidly (hauling them in with his arms, as it were), one after another, thrusting his beak into the tube of each. It takes him but a moment to dispatch one. It is a singular sight, a humblebee clambering over a bed of these delicate flowers."

To facilitate pollination, this little plant produces two types of blossoms: one has the pollen-bearing stamens in the bottom part of the flower tube and two stigmas sticking out into the open air; the other type has the stigmas below and the stamens above the mouth of the corolla. More than bumblebees are busy in the bluets, for small bees, various hoverflies, and even butterflies feed at and pollinate these flowers. The orange-and-brown-patterned wings of the meadow fritillary (*Clossiana bellona*) combine beautifully with the blue of the petals.

> *Houstonias. How affecting that, annually at this season, as surely as the sun takes a higher course in the heavens, this pure and simple little flower peeps out and spots the great globe with white in our America, its four little white or bluish petals on a slender stalk making a delicate flower about a third of an inch in diameter! What a significant, though faint, utterance of spring through the veins of earth! Dewey calls it Venus' Pride. Gray says truly, "a very delicate little herb, . . . producing in spring a profusion of handsome bright blue blossoms fading to white, with a yellow eye." I should say bluish-white.* —April 21, 1853

Later, Thoreau speaks of bluets whitening the fields a quarter of a mile off, claiming they are to the sere, brown grass what the shadbush is to the brown and bare spout-lands or young woods.

Alice Morse Earle wrote that bluets are "a milky way of minute stars," and Louise Beebe Wilder writes this grand description in her book *The Rock Garden:* "Houstonia is a most precious small native, the daintiest and most engaging of fairies—and sometimes the most elusive. Not by any means are these little Quaker Ladies to be led by the nose. In some places they will dwell and in some they will not. We may set them out in a pleasantly shaded and cool spot, but we need not be surprised if the next season this choice locality is quite deserted, and to find away along the edges of the starved paths, on precarious ledges, or from the midst of tight wads of Saxifrages, in all sorts of unexpected places, little gatherings of demure Quaker Ladies, quite gleeful and heady with liberty. Gradually they will increase, choosing their own neighborhoods, until there are throngs of the charming creatures, and one is glad to be alive just to look at them."

The true or common bluet, *Houstonia caerulea,* grows in tufts, with leafy stems, each tipped with one flower. The creeping bluet, *H. michauxii* (*H. serpyllifolia*), has stems covered with small round leaves, and the flower stalks begin from the leaf axils, standing erect. The older species name refers to the resemblance of the leaves to creeping thyme, a plant once called *Serpyllum.*

Most botanists do not agree on the names of the three taller members of the genus, *Houstonia lanceolata, H. longifolia,* and *H. tenuifolia,* which are sometimes lumped together as varieties of *H. purpurea.* They grow to eighteen inches, and the white to purple flowers, borne in terminal cymes, have a longer floral tube and slightly smaller lobes than *H. caerulea.* Even when many plants bloom together, they lack the impact of a field of common bluets.

According to Neltje Blanchan, one day in January, John Burroughs found a single bluet blooming outside Washington, in earth that was frozen solid. One winter, I removed a patch of bluets before the ground froze, and placed them in a cool terrarium. The plants burst into bloom in early March. *The Royal Horticultural Dictionary of Gardening* (not the new high-priced edition) says that common bluets make a good pot plant for the alpine house and are also used to cover the surface of pots that hold bare-stemmed hardy plants, much like mosses would be used. They even have a medicinal use: the Cherokees used a tea made from bluets to treat bed-wetting.

THE WATER FLOWERS

I am glad to have drunk water so long, as I prefer the natural sky to an opium-eater's heaven. . . . [I] would keep sober always, and lead a sane life not indebted to stimulants. It is the only drink of a wise man, and only the foolish habitually use any other.   *—Summer 1850*

Thoreau was thirty-three when he wrote the above thoughts on water. But he thought of water in other ways, too. The same year that he spoke of water's part in a healthy lifestyle, he also noted its esthetic virtues:

A field of water betrays the spirit that is in the air. It has new life and motion. It is intermediate between land and sky. On land, only the grass and trees wave, but the water itself is rippled by the wind. I see the breeze dash across it in streaks and flakes of light.   *—Summer 1850*

Later, in 1851, he noted how valuable water was by moonlight as it reflected the light with a faint, glimmering sheen. In the spring of the year, he thought, water shone with an inward light like a heaven on earth.

The silent depth and serenity and majesty of water! Strange that men should distinguish gold and diamonds, when these precious elements are so common. I saw a distant river by moonlight, making no noise, yet flowing, as by day, still to sea, like melted silver reflecting the moonlight. Far away it lay encircling the earth.   *—June 11, 1851*

The American Water Lily
Nymphaea odorata

Style: Floating aquatic plants of great beauty, usually flowering from early morning until noon. **Leaves:** Round leaves often ten inches across float on the water's surface. **Flowers:** Lovely, fragrant white or pink double flowers up to five inches across, with numerous yellow stamens. **Zone:** 4. **Uses:** Mandatory in the water garden. **Culture:** Warm shallow ponds with a minimum of a half day's sun.

How could it stand these heats? It has pantingly opened, and now lies stretched out by its too long stem on the surface of the shrunken river. The air grows more and more blue, making pretty effects when one wood is seen from another through a little interval. Some pigeons here are resting in the thickest of the white pines during the heat of the day, migrating, no doubt. They are unwilling to move for me. Flies buzz and rain about my hat, and the dead twigs and leaves of the white pine, which the choppers have left here, exhale a dry and almost sickening scent. —*July 21, 1851*

IT WAS A HOT DAY IN JULY WHEN THOREAU FIRST MENTIONED THE FRA-grant water lily. He didn't document the day's temperature but at 10 A.M. simply asked how the flower could put up with that heat. That's one of the beauties of growing water lilies: no matter how hot it gets, they adapt to the heat. Unlike terrestrial plants, they can never give off more water than they take in.

The water lily usually chosen for wild gardens and large pond plantings is the fragrant water lily, or *Nymphaea odorata*. The genus name is from the Greek *nymphe* and in this case, because of the habitat, means a water nymph. Other common names include the sweet-scented white water lily, pond lily, water nymph, and the water cabbage.

In my experience, nothing is so opposed to poetry—not crime—as business. It is a negation of life. . . . The wind exposes the red under sides of the white lily pads. This is one of the aspects of the river now. The bud-bearing stem of this plant is a little larger, but otherwise like the leaf-stem, and coming directly from the long, large root. . . . How much mud and water are required to support their vitality! It is pleasant to remember these quiet Sabbath mornings by remote stagnant rivers and ponds, where pure white water-lilies, just expanded, not yet infested by insects, float on the waveless

water and perfume the atmosphere. Nature never appears
more serene and innocent and fragrant. A hundred white
lilies, open to the sun, rest on the surface smooth as oil amid
their pads, while devil's-needles are glancing over them.

—*June 29, 1852*

Three days later, Thoreau borrowed a boat from Brigham, the wheelwright, who, according to the journal, "understands that I am abroad for viewing the works of Nature and not loafing, though he makes the pursuit a semi-religious one—." A talkative character at the nearby bridge asked Thoreau as he unlocked the boat, "Do you know anything that is good for the rheumatism?" Thoreau answered and later recorded in his journal that "I had heard of so many and had so little faith in any that I had forgotten them all."

Soon Thoreau was rowing down the river parting the white lilies in all their splendor, all fully open, sometimes with their lower petals resting directly on the water's surface. The largest appeared to grow in the shallow water, where some stood five or six inches out of water and were five inches in diameter. He examined two blossoms that each had twenty-nine petals.

Then he pushed the boat into the midst of a shallow bay, where the water, about a foot deep, was covered with lily pads, and hundreds more lilies had just opened.

[They] were a pearly white, and though the water amid the
pads was quite unrippled, the passing air gave a slight oscil-
lating, boat-like motion to and fro to the flowers, like boats
held fast by their cables. Some of the lilies had a beautiful
rosaceous tinge, most conspicuous in the half-opened flower,
extending through the calyx to the second row of petals, on
those parts of the petals between the calyx-leaves which
were most exposed to the influence of the light. They were
tinged with red, as they are very commonly tinged with

*green, as if there were a gradual transition from the stamens
to the petals.*

*The form of this flower is also very perfect, the petals
are so distinctly arranged at equal intervals and at all
angles, from nearly a perpendicular to horizontal about the
center.*   *—July 2, 1852*

At this place in the journal there is a small pen-and-ink sketch
of a flower viewed from the side.

After eating his lunch at Rice's landing, Thoreau observed that
every white lily in the river was shut, "and they remained so all the
afternoon, though it was no more sunny nor cloudy than the
forenoon," except some that he had picked before noon, then cast
into the river; floating along, lodged amid the pondweed, these
had apparently lost the ability to close their petals and remained
open.

Back on the river on the morning of July 4, 1852, Thoreau cut
off a dozen perfect lily buds that had not opened and took them
home. Filling a large pan with water, he cut the flower stems very
short. Then he turned back their calyx leaves with his fingers so
that they could float upright. With his warm fingers, he touched
the points of the petals, blew upon them, then tossed the lilies into
the water. Most of the flowers opened immediately, the rest gradually over the course of an hour or two.

By 12:30 P.M., the lilies began to close, but they continued to
both open and close in the house for five days until the stamens
had shed their pollen, turned rusty, and started to decay. Now the
beauty of the flower was gone. "It is remarkable that those flowers
which are most emblematical of purity should grow in the mud,"
Thoreau wrote.

The chief pollinators of our native white water lilies are bees
and flower flies, although an occasional beetle or skipper butterfly
will alight. The dragonflies that approach are looking for the small
gnats that ramble around the stamens.

There are medicinal uses, too. The American Indians made a root tea for coughs, tuberculosis, mouth sores, inflamed glands, and bowel complaints. A root poultice was used for swellings.

In *Flowers and Plants* (New York: Quandrangle, 1974), Robert Shosteck writes that cooking the unopened flower buds for a few minutes in boiling water makes a palatable dish when properly seasoned, and the young, unopened leaves chopped up and boiled for several minutes can be added with good effect to stews and soups.

When it comes to growing fragrant water lilies in the home pool or tub, begin by planting the roots in a six-inch clay flower-pot, using plain old garden soil and a handful of bulb food. Cover the root to the crown, pack the soil, then add a layer of gravel to the top. Saturate the pot, then lower it into the pool or pond—the gravel will help to keep the water clean. The pot's surface should be at least a foot under the water's surface.

These water lilies are hardy way up north because the roots are protected from freezing by a blanket of unfrozen water. If frozen, the roots will die. You can leave the pots out in your pond through the winter if the bottom stays above 32° F. If it does not, remove the pots and keep them in a cool place through the winter, checking that the soil stays evenly moist.

The Spatterdock, or Great Yellow Lily
Nuphar advena

Style: Floating aquatic plants with flowers resembling waxy yellow bowls on thick stems. **Leaves:** Large oval leaves, sometimes a foot across, either float on the water's surface or stand slightly above. **Flowers:** Six yellow sepals surrounded by numerous stamens resemble terrestrial globeflowers (*Trollius* spp.). **Zone:** 4. **Uses:** Of great interest in the water garden. **Culture:** Warm shallow ponds with a minimum of a half day's sun.

THE COMMON NAME OF SPATTERDOCK OR COW LILY MAY TELL YOU THAT this particular water plant is considered to be less beautiful than fragrant water lilies, but it, too, has a place in the water garden. *Nuphar* is from the Arabic vernacular name for this plant, and *advena* means "newly arrived." The species name refers to spatterdock's arrival in England in 1772. The common name is supposed to refer to a docklike plant that spatters its ripe seeds. In England these plants are called brandy-bottle and frog-lilies.

Thoreau mentions these plants a number of times throughout the seasons. Early in spring 1853, he found the yellow bud of a *Nuphar advena* in a ditch on the turnpike, its bud "nearly half an inch in diameter on a very thick stem, three fourths of an inch thick at base and ten inches long, four or five inches above the mud. This may have swollen somewhat during the warmest weather in the winter after pushing up in the fall."

His most imaginative description of this plant came late in October 1855, when he saw the roots of the great yellow lily lying on the mud near a ditch in the meadow dug by potters collecting the gray mud. Some of the roots were three and a half inches in diameter, with their great eyes or protuberant shoulders where the leaf stalks stood in quincunxial order (an arrangement of five stalks, four making a square with one in the square's center). "What rank vigor they suggest! Like serpents winding amid the mud of the meadow."

The sepals of a spatterdock flower pretend to be petals, using their yellow as a come-on to insects. The very small petals are inside the large sepals, arranged around the anthers. At first only the sticky stigma is revealed, ready to receive pollen from another flower, the anthers remaining enclosed. In a day or two, the pollen ripens and the fertilized flower opens, exposing the anthers. In this way self-fertilization is avoided. A few hours spent in watching the flowers reveals that insect visitors include small bees, beetles, and flies.

Thoreau also described the fruit of the spatterdock, noting

that in mid-September, he saw green and purplish fruit ripening underwater. He included a sketch in the journal and also a sketch of one of the many yellow seeds.

Medicinal uses include a root tea used by the American Indians for "sexual irritability," chills accompanied by a fever, various wounds, contusions, and boils. It's also a folk remedy for impotence. But authorities warn that large doses of the root could be potentially toxic.

Spatterdock is a spreader and only suited for a large pond with water at least two feet deep. Purchase roots in the spring, and, using a few rocks, peg them to the pond bottom until they gain purchase.

The Marsh Marigold, or Cowslip
Caltha palustris

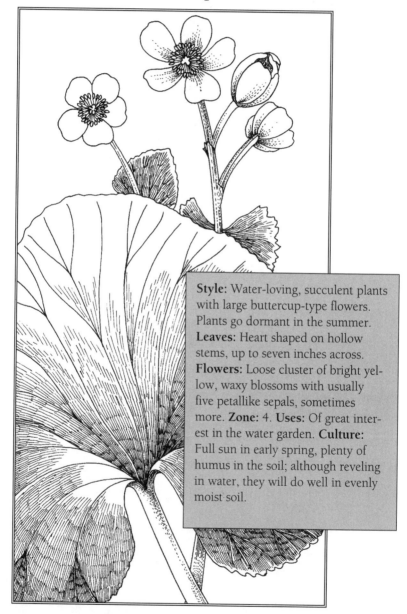

Style: Water-loving, succulent plants with large buttercup-type flowers. Plants go dormant in the summer. **Leaves:** Heart shaped on hollow stems, up to seven inches across. **Flowers:** Loose cluster of bright yellow, waxy blossoms with usually five petallike sepals, sometimes more. **Zone:** 4. **Uses:** Of great interest in the water garden. **Culture:** Full sun in early spring, plenty of humus in the soil; although reveling in water, they will do well in evenly moist soil.

*I am surprised to find the cowslip in full bloom at the Second
Division meadow, numerous flowers. Growing in the water,
it is not, comparatively, so backward this year perhaps. Its
heart or kidney shaped, crenate leaves, which had not
freshly grown when I was here before, have suddenly pushed
up.* —April 25, 1852

*The mottled sunlight and shade, seen looking into the
woods, is more like summer. But the season is more forward
at the Second Division Brook, where the cowslip is in blossom,—these bright yellow suns of the meadow in rich clusters, their flowers contrasting with the green leaves, from
amidst the all-producing, dark-bottomed water. A flower-
fire bursting up, as though in crevices in the meadow. They
are very rich, seen in the meadow where they grow, and the
most conspicuous flower at present, but held in the hand are
rather coarse. But their yellow and green are really rich,
and in the meadow they are the most delicate objects. Their
bright yellow is something incredible when first beheld.*
—April 29, 1852

FOR MANY SPRINGS, MY WALKS AROUND OUR COUNTRY HOME IN UPSTATE
New York followed a dirt road for about a half mile to an abandoned
field. I would walk along a winding fieldstone wall to a place where
stones had tumbled on the ground, then take a pathway shaded by
old hemlocks and white pines for a mile and end up in a grand
swamp. Here the waters continually bubbled with decaying vegetation, and the wildflowers bloomed from early spring. Every
April, in an area of water surrounded by newly emerged ferns,
where fallen trees crisscrossed the calm surface, I was always surprised to find the cowslips in full bloom.

Almost every year in April, Thoreau wrote in his journal about
his encounters with marsh marigolds. At the Second Division

Meadow, for example, numerous golden flowers appeared spring after spring. One cowslip, he noted, was slow in opening but it would be out by the next day. "How they improve their time! Not a moment of sunshine lost. One thing I may depend on: there is no idling with the flowers. They advance steadily as the clock."

Thoreau often wrote of the cowslip's vigorous growth and how, early in the spring, it makes the best show of any flower.

> *Leaf, stem, bud, and flower are all very handsome in their place and season. It has no scent but speaks wholly to the eye. The petals are covered at base with a transparent, dew-like, apparently golden nectar. Better for yellows than for green.*   *—May 4, 1852*

Common names include meadow-gowan, American cowslip, king-cup, May-blob, *souci d'eau,* and meadowbright. *Caltha,* the Latin name for a strong-scented yellow flower, was mistakenly applied to this wildflower. Cowslip is a polite way of saying "cowslop," a place where cows have contributed organic offerings to fertility. *Palustris* means "of swamps." The plants are found from Labrador to Alaska, south to North Carolina, then west to Tennessee, Iowa, and Nebraska.

Cowslip blooms too early in the year to be pollinated by crowds of honeybees. Even the new bumblebees have yet to hatch and mature and the present visitors are those looking for food before starting new nests. A number of flies, little beetles, and tiny bugs are attracted by the smell of its nectar, but the usual pollinators are the Syrphidae, or flower flies. Some are brilliantly colored and some covered with fuzz like bees, but they are harmless feeders on pollen and nectar that endure fertilitzation as they crawl around the flowers.

> *There, in the slow, muddy brook near the head of Well Meadow, within a few rods of its source, where it winds amid*

the alders, which shelter the plants somewhat, while they are open enough now to admit the sun, I find two cowslips in full bloom, shedding pollen; and they may have opened two or three days ago; for I saw many conspicuous buds there on the second which now I do not see. Have they not been eaten off? Do we not often lose the earliest flowers thus?

—April 8, 1856

We certainly do. And the cowslip asks for it because it has great edible qualities. In spring, or close to the flowering season, cowslips are used both as a potherb and as cooked garden greens. The leaves and stems are brought to a boil, drained, then brought to a boil again, a procedure necessary to remove poisonous glucosides. They are served like spinach and, in many parts of the country, the tender flower buds are pickled and used as a substitute for capers. Here again the buds must be cooked first. In *Edible Wild Plants,* Oliver Medsger suggests this recipe: take cooked cowslips, add salt, drain, and chop fine. To a saucepan, add a teaspoon of butter plus a tablespoon of flour, then mix, adding salt and pepper to taste. Add the greens and one-half cup of cream or rich milk, stir until well mixed, and serve. If you gather cowslips, make sure you do not take either the false or white hellebore (*Veratrum viride*) or the water hemlock (*Conium maculatum*), since both are deadly poison.

Northeasterners once mixed maple syrup with a tea made of cowslip and used it as a cough syrup. The tea was also used as a laxative and as an antidote to snake venom. People with sensitive skin should be careful when handling this plant because all parts can irritate mucous membranes and skin. A yellow dye can be made from the flower's sepals.

The Arrowheads
Sagittaria latifolia

Style: Aquatic plants with arrow-head-shaped leaves and attractive white flowers. **Leaves:** Most members of the genus have leaves shaped like arrowheads, some wide, some narrow, but usually about twenty inches long. **Flowers:** White with three petals and three green sepals with numerous stamens and pistils. **Zone:** 4. **Uses:** Very beautiful in the water garden. **Culture:** Warm, shallow ponds and stream margins with a minimum of a half day's sun.

ONE MID-AUGUST AFTERNOON IN 1851, THOREAU WENT WALKING along a small stream to a damp meadow and found an arrowhead plant. In his journal he wrote, "It has very little root that I can find to eat," the only mention he made in his journal about using arrowheads as food. The American Indians, however, were well acquainted with the tuberous roots of arrowheads, boiling them like potatoes, or sometimes roasting them in hot ashes. Lewis and Clark found native tribes living at the mouth of Oregon's Multnomah River, now called the Willamette, using these roots, which they called wapatoo, as a mainstay of their diets.

The *Journals of Lewis and Clark* mentions "purchas[ing] from an old squaw, for armbands and rings, a few wapatoo roots, on which we subsisted. They are nearly equal in flavor to the Irish potato and afford a very good substitute for bread."

According to Bradford Angier, wading Indians would use their toes or sticks to dislodge the roots, allowing the tubers to rise quickly to the surface. The Chinese who were brought to America for cheap railroad labor in the West adopted the wapatoo as a favorite food, calling it the tule potato, and brought it to commercial markets. Common names of the arrowheads include duck potato, swan potato, katniss, tule potato, and swamp potato. The name *Sagittaria* is from the Latin word *sagitta*, an arrow, and refers to the shape of the leaf in most species. Distribution ranges from Nova Scotia to British Columbia and south to Florida and Mexico.

My wife uses arrowroot in the kitchen. When I asked her about this powdered form of the tuber, she gave me her copy of *Joy of Cooking*, by Irma S. Rombauer (Indianapolis: Bobbs-Merrill, 1964). There under *arrowroot* I read, "Of all the thickeners, this makes the most delicately textured sauces. But use it only when the sauce is to be served within ten minutes of thickening. It will not hold, nor will it reheat. Since the flavor of arrowroot is neutral and it does not have to be cooked to remove rawness, as do flour and cornstarch, and since it thickens at a lower temperature than either of them, it is ideal for use in egg and other sauces which should not boil."

In addition to eating them, the American Indians made a tea from the tubers for indigestion and made poultices of them to treat various wounds and sores. A leaf tea was prepared for rheumatism, and sometimes a poultice of leaves was used to stop milk production after birth.

In July 1852, Thoreau rendered small drawings that he dubbed "rude outline sketches" to portray the common form of the arrowhead, noted for its large, clear white flowers. To him, the sagittaria had a breezy air with its shiny three-petaled flowers.

> *There is also the exquisite beauty of the small sagittaria,*
> *which I find out, maybe a day or two,—three transparent*
> *crystalline white petals with a yellow eye and as many small*
> *purplish calyx-leaves, four or five inches above the same*
> *mud.*   *—June 19, 1853*

According to botanical journals past and present, there are some thirty species widely distributed in temperate and tropical regions, all rooted aquatics. The leaves are all basal with stems usually as tall as the water is deep, although there are some submerged leaf forms that are really modified stems without leaf blades. The species usually found in American waters is *Sagittaria latifolia,* called *S. variabilis* by Asa Gray because of its variable leaf shape. In most species the upper flowers have stamens with or without pistils, while the lower flowers possess only pistils. Thus the genus can be described as monoecious, having unisexual flowers on the same plant, dioecious, with unisexual flowers on separate plants, or hermaphroditic, that is, bisexual plants having both types of flowers.

Five years passed before Thoreau again mentioned arrowheads.

> *Stop[ping] by the culvert opposite the centaurea, to look at*
> *the sagittaria leaves. Perhaps this plant is in its prime (?). Its*
> *leaves vary remarkably in form. I see, in a thick patch six or*
> *eight feet in diameter, leaves nearly a foot long . . . and*

others, as long or longer, . . . with all the various intermedi-
ate ones. The very narrow ones, perhaps, around the edge of
the patch, being also of a darker green, are not distinguished
at first, but mistaken for grass.   —*August 26, 1858*

Arrowheads are beautifully adapted to their aquatic environment. The flowers rise into the open air and attract pollinators,
and buried in the mud below, the starchy tubers receive nutrients
and oxygen from the leaves. The leaves above the water have
plenty of surface area for photosynthesis; those below the surface
have a shape that allows them to slice through the water without
being torn to shreds by the currents. On a warm day toward the
end of August 1859, on the way to Walden, Thoreau again wrote
about arrowheads:

The arrowhead is still a common flower and an important
one. I see some very handsome ones in Cardinal Ditch,
whose corollas are an inch and a half in diameter. The
greater part, however, have gone to seed. The flowers I see at
present are autumn flowers, such as have risen above the
stubble in shorn fields since it was cut, whose tops have
commonly been clipped by the scythe or the cow; of the late
flowers, as asters and goldenrods, which grow in neglected
fields and along ditches and hedgerows. —August 27, 1859

The Whirligig Beetles

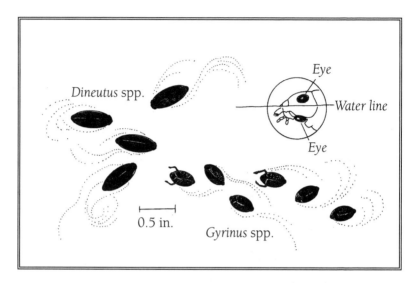

I see the northern lights over my shoulder, to remind me of the Esquimaux and that they are still my contemporaries on this globe, that they too are taking their walks on another part of the planet, in pursuit of seals, perchance. The stars are dimly reflected in the water. The path of water-bugs in the moon's rays is like ripples of light. . . . I hear no frogs these nights,—bullfrogs or others,—as in the spring. It is not the season of sound. —September 7, 1851

GARDENERS GENERALLY EXERCISE LITTLE CONTROL OVER THE INSECTS THAT visit their gardens. It's possible to buy praying mantids, green lacewings, or ladybugs to add to the garden environment but there's no guarantee they will stay in the neighborhood.

Thoreau spent many pages describing water bugs, and because their antics are delightful to watch, they should be encouraged to stay in the water garden's vicinity.

On a warm day late in January, while walking at Nut Meadow Brook, Thoreau wrote that the small water bugs were as abundant and active as in summer.

> *I see forty or fifty circling together in the smooth and sunny bays all along the brook. This is something new to me. What must they think of this winter? It is like a child waked up and set to playing at midnight. Methinks they are more ready to dive to the bottom when disturbed than usual. At night, of course, they dive to the bottom and bury themselves, and if in the morning they perceive no curtain of ice drawn over their sky, and the pleasant weather continues, they gladly rise again and resume their gyrations in some sunny bay amid the alders and the stubble. But I fear for their nervous systems, lest this be too much activity, too much excitement. The sun falling thus warmly for so long on the open surface of the brook tempts them upward gradually, till there is a little group gyrating there as in summer. What a funny way they have of going to bed! They do not take a light and retire upstairs; they go below. Suddenly it is heels up and heads down, and they go down to their muddy bed and let the unresting stream flow over them in their dream. . . . What a deep slumber must be theirs, and what dreams, down in the mud there! . . . I see one chasing a mote, and the wave the creature makes always causes the mote to float away from it. I would like to know what it is they communicate to one another, they who appear to value each other's society so much. How many water bugs make a quorum? What is their precise hour for retiring?* —January 24, 1858

The water bugs that Thoreau described are called whirligig beetles. The large whirligig beetles (*Dineutus* spp.) are oval, black beetles from an eighth to five-eighths of an inch across that glide across the quiet waters of ponds, lakes, and slow-moving streams in summer and on into fall. The small whirligigs (*Gyrinus* spp.) measure about a quarter inch across.

Thoreau mentions catching a handful of small water bugs, perhaps fifteen or twenty, each about the size of an apple seed, which is what some people call them because of their scent. Thoreau's not so sure the smell is of apples. Dr. Frank E. Lutz, author of *The Field Book of Insects* (New York: G. P. Putnam & Sons, 1948) and curator of the department of entomology at the American Museum of Natural History, reports that when disturbed, whirligig beetles will squeak and give off a fluid that is sometimes described as ill smelling and other times as smelling of apples. He notes that about the beginning of August, the larvae creep out of the water (they resemble small centipedes), climb up the stems of water plants, and spin a gray cocoon that is pointed at both ends. The adult whirligigs emerge a few weeks later. As the weather gets colder, they hibernate at the bottom of ponds and streams, but they will come out during mild winter weather for what Dr. Lutz calls (and I believe Thoreau would agree) midwinter dances.

These whirling dervishes of the water world have compound eyes that are divided into upper and lower parts so that the insects can see both above and below the water's surface simultaneously. Their short antennae bear two specialized scooplike segments and six clubbed segments. With these antennae, whirligigs are able to detect wavelets in the surface film of the water so that they can avoid obstacles and each other and find prey.

In addition to whirligigs, Thoreau's Garden needs water striders, which Thoreau mentioned once in the journal, on a mild winter day in late December.

> *At the turnpike bridge, water stands a foot or two deep over the ice. Water spiders have come out and are skating against the stream. How much they depend on January thaws!*
> —December 28, 1851

Common water striders *(Gerris remigis)* are also called water spiders, water darters, and, in Texas, Jesus bugs because they walk on water. They are slender insects, not spiders, with long bodies and even longer middle and hind legs that enable them to dart around on the surface of ponds, slow creeks, and other quiet waters. The shadows they cast below their bodies show small dimples on the water's surface where their feet touch. Surface tension and their specially adapted feet allow them to dart about on the water's surface as though they were wearing skates. Striders are found throughout North America, feeding on small water life that floats up from below or tiny insects that fall from above. They overwinter under fallen leaves near the water's edge.

PUFFBALLS AND EARTHSTARS
The Puffballs

THOREAU VISITED THE HUCKLEBERRY PASTURE ON THE LEE FARM NEAR Nawshawtuct, or Lee's Hill, and described the mushrooms he found there:

> By the fence of old barn boards, I notice many little pale-brown dome-shaped (puckered to a centre beneath) puffballs, which emit their dust. When you pinch them, a smoke-like brown dust (snuff-colored) issues from the orifice at their top, just like smoke from a chimney. It is so fine and light that it rises into the air and is wafted away like smoke. They are low Oriental domes or mosques. Sometimes crowded together in nests, like a collection of humble cottages on the moor, in the coal-pit or Numidian style; for there is suggested some humble hearth beneath, from which this smoke comes up, as it were the homes of slugs and crickets. They please me not a little by their resemblance to rude dome-shaped, turf-built cottages on the plain, wherein some humble but everlasting life is lived. Amid the low and withering grass or the stubble there they are gathered, and their smoke ascends between the legs of the herds and the traveler. I imagine a hearth and pot, and some snug but humble family passing its Sunday evening beneath each one. —October 4, 1856

I suspect that somewhere there is a dedicated gardener who could grow puffballs on demand, but I suspect it's beyond the reach of most of us. These fascinating funguses (fungi is the Latin plural) are commonly called pouch funguses because they all keep their spores in closed chambers until ready to be dispersed. The closed chamber is called a *gleba* (from the Latin word for clod), and the glebae are surrounded by a rind called a *peridium* (derived from the Greek word for a leather wallet), which, depending on the puffball involved, has a characteristic way of opening up to allow the spores to escape to the world. Puff balls, along with stinkhorns and earthstars, belong to a large group of funguses called Gasteromycetes, or stomach funguses.

149

The plant part of the puffball consists of mycelial threads that form an extensive underground network of white fibers in the decaying vegetable matter in which they grow. Because of this habit, they are often called subterranean saprophytes. As the time to spore approaches, little balls appear on the white threads and begin to increase in size. When ready to scatter spores, the puffballs emerge from the ground and passersby know of their existence. Even today, most rural children have pinched these encrusted marshmallows to see the smoke rise, hardly knowing that they were scattering the spores of a new generation to the wind.

Some when you press them harder, emit clear water—the relics of rain or dew—along with the dust, which last, however, has no affinity for it, but is quite dry and smoke-like. I locate there at once all that is simple and admirable in human life. There is no virtue which their roots exclude. I imagine with what contentment and faith I could come home to them at evening. I see some not yet ripe, still entire and rounded at top. When I break them open, they are found to be quite soggy, of a stringy white consistency, almost cream-like, riper and yellowish at top, where they will burst by and by. On one I find a slug feeding, with a little hole beneath him, and a cricket has eaten out the whole inside of another in which he is housed. This before they are turned to dust. Large chocolate-colored ones have long since burst and are spread out wide like a shallow dish.   —October 4, 1856

Young puffballs have a fleshy interior and some species are considered gourmet items, especially when sliced and fried in butter. Many are termed inedible, a few are outright poisonous, and more than a few are so unappetizing to the eye that they could hardly appeal to the stomach.

The fleshy interior gradually turns yellow or pinkish, then darkens and dries until most of it is filled with the dustlike spores. Then the rind breaks and the spores escape.

On December 6, 1852, another Indian summer day, Thoreau saw some puffballs in the woods, "wonderfully full of sulphur-like dust, which yellowed my shoes, greenish-yellow." And in September of the next year, "puffballs, now four inches through, turned dark from white, and ripe, fill the air with dust four or five feet high when I kick them."

In *The Mushroom Book* (New York: Doubleday, Page & Company, 1914), Nina L. Marshall describes the opening of these globes: "Sometimes the wall breaks off in scales; sometimes it is punctured at the summit with one hole, sometimes with several, and sometimes it splits and turns back to form a star on the ground. Sometimes the balls contain elastic threads (capillitum), which help to push out the spores, and sometimes they do not. Sometimes there are threads massed at the base without spores in them, so that they form a sterile base of sterile subgleba, and sometimes the threads are massed to form a central column on the interior of the ball."

I see one of those great ash-colored puffballs with a tinge of purple, open like a cup, four inches in diameter. The upper surface is (as if it were bleached) quite hoary. Though it is but just brought to light from beneath the deep snow, and the last two days have been misty or rainy without sun, it is just as dry and dusty as ever, and the drops of water rest on it, at first undetected, being covered with its dust, looking like unground pearls. I brought it home and held it in a basin of water. To my surprise, when held under water it looked like a mass of silver or melted lead, it was so coated with air, and when I suffered it to rise,—for it had to be kept down by force,—instead of being heavy like a sponge which has soaked water, it was as light as a feather, and its surface perfectly dry, and when touched it gave out its dust the same as ever. It was impossible to wet. It seems to be encased in a silvery coat of air which is water-tight. The water did not penetrate into it at all, and running off as you lifted it up, it was just as dry as before, and on the least jar floating in dust above your head. —February 8, 1857

The Cup-shaped Puffball
Calvatia cyathiformis

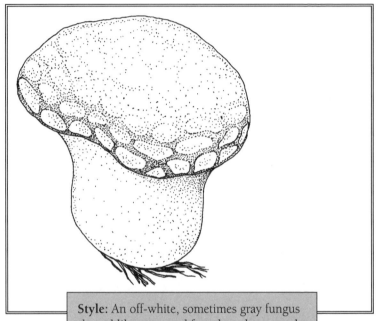

Style: An off-white, sometimes gray fungus shaped like a top and found on the ground in meadows and pastures. **Bark or outer coat:** Thin, smooth, and easily peeled off. **Spores:** Violet to dark purple. **Edibility:** Edible and good.

THOREAU'S PUFFBALL PROBABLY WAS THE CUP-SHAPED PUFFBALL, A SPECIES with a sphere of two to six inches in diameter. These puffballs are found throughout eastern North America in open fields and lawns. Left after the spores are dispersed, the large violet-brown cuplike base can often be seen throughout the winter and persists even under the snow.

The Giant Puffball
Calvatia maxima

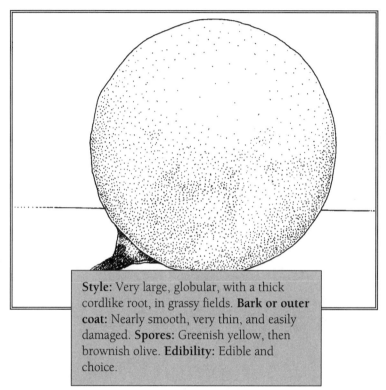

Style: Very large, globular, with a thick cordlike root, in grassy fields. **Bark or outer coat:** Nearly smooth, very thin, and easily damaged. **Spores:** Greenish yellow, then brownish olive. **Edibility:** Edible and choice.

THE GIANT PUFFBALL WAS KNOWN AS *LYCOPERDON GIGANTEUM* OR *L. MAXIMA* in Thoreau's day. They are still sold at farmers' markets in the fall. They range from baseball size up to eighteen inches in diameter or more, the larger sizes having the best texture. Buyers and collectors are advised to section the specimen to check for pinholes that indicate the presence of worms and to be sure the gleba has not started to turn yellow. It has been estimated that the largest of these puffballs contain approximately one hundred sixty billion spores.

In colonial times, the dried, spongy threads were used as tinder to catch the sparks that flew from the flintstone when it was struck. And Thoreau notes a medicinal use:

> *The puffball is used by doctors to stop bleeding. Has not this property to do with its power of repelling moisture? Some have now almost entirely lost their dust, leaving a dry almost woolly substance.* —February 20, 1857

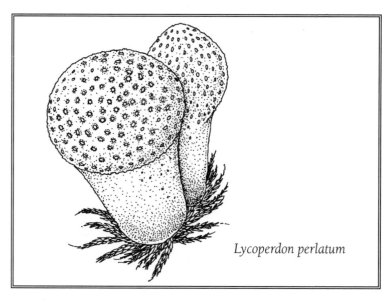

Lycoperdon perlatum

There are other members of the puffball family about which Thoreau makes no note in his journal. *Lycoperdon perlatum* is covered with cone-shaped protuberances on its upper surface, making it look like a sea urchin that has lost its spines. Usually about three inches in diameter, it's common in the late summer and fall wherever there are forests or accumulated woody debris like sawdust.

The hard-skinned puffballs are a dingy, brownish yellow and

resemble pale leather. The pattern of warts on their surface is used in field identifications.

> *[I found] many of those pale-brown roughish fungi (it looks like Loudon's plate of* Scleroderma, *perhaps* verrucosum), *two or three inches in diameter. Those which are ripe are so softened at the top as to admit the rain through the skin (as well as after it opens), and the interior is shaking like a jelly, and if you open it you see what looks like a yellowish gum or jelly amid the dark fuscous fist, but it is this water colored by the dust; yet when they are half full of water they emit dust nevertheless. They are in various states, from a firm, hard and dry unopen[ed] to a half-empty and flabby moist cup.*
>
> —*October 25, 1860*

Scleroderma aurantium

The puffball Thoreau described is probably *Scleroderma aurantium*, the commonest of the hard-skinned puffballs, with fruits from one to three inches in diameter. Some books claim it's edible. But Alexander Smith warns in *The Mushroom Hunter's Field Guide* (Ann Arbor: The University of Michigan Press, 1966) that *Scleroderma aurantium* is "not recommended here. It would seem to be low grade at best."

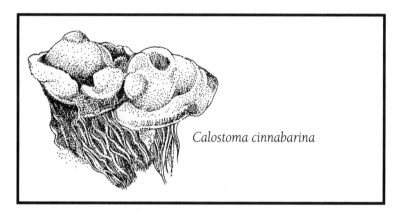

Calostoma cinnabarina

Another member of the puffball group is the stalked puffball-in-aspic *(Calostoma cinnabarina)*, a fungus with a bright red spore sac covered with a thick clear jelly and sitting atop a spongy red stem. Field guide entries for it usually conclude, "Edibility unknown"; after all, who would want to try it!

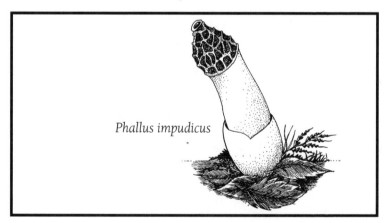

Phallus impudicus

The stinkhorns are usually represented by bizarre *Phallus ravenelii* or the equally fantastic *P. impudicus*, both of which attract flies and other insects with their odor. Thoreau called these last funguses offensive and recorded his views of *Phallus impudicus:*

*Found amid the sphagnum on the dry bank on the south side
of the Turnpike, just below Everett's meadow, a rare and
remarkable fungus, such as I have heard of but never seen
before. The whole height six and three quarters inches, two
thirds of it being buried in the sphagnum. It may be divided
into three parts, pileus, stem, and base,—or scrotum, for it
is a perfect phallus. One of those fungi named* impudicus,
*I think. In all respects a most disgusting object, yet very
suggestive. It is hollow from top to bottom, the form of the
hollow answering to that of the outside. The color of the outside white excepting the pileus, which is olive-colored and
somewhat coarsely corrugated, with an oblong mouth at tip
about one and three eighths inches high by one and a half
wide. The stem (bare portion) is three inches long . . . horizontally viewed of an oval form. Longest diameter at base
one and a half inches, at top (on edge of pileus) fifteen
sixteenths of an inch. Short diameters in both cases about
two thirds of as much. It is a delicate white cylinder of a
finely honeycombed and crispy material about three sixteenths of an inch thick, or more, the whole very straight and
regular. The base, or scrotum, is of an irregular bag form,
about one inch by two in the extremes, consisting of a thick
trembling gelatinous mass surrounding the bottom of the
stem and covered with a tough white skin of a darker tint
than the stem. The whole plant rather frail and trembling.
There was at first a very thin delicate white collar (or volva?)
about the base of the stem above the scrotum. It was offensive to the eye as to the scent, the cap rapidly melting and
defiling what it touched with a fetid, olivaceous, semiliquid
matter. In an hour or two the plant scented the whole house
wherever placed, so that it could not be endured. I was afraid
to sleep in my chamber where it had lain until the room had
been well ventilated. It smelled like a dead rat in the ceiling,
in all the ceilings of the house. Pray, what was Nature think-*

ing of when she made this? She almost puts herself on a level with those who draw in privies. The cap had at first a smooth and almost dry surface, of a sort of olive slate-color, but the next day this colored surface all melted out, leaving deep corrugations or gills—rather honeycomb-like cells—with a white bottom. —October 16, 1856

The Earthstars

By the path, and in the sandy field beyond, are many of those star-fingered puffballs. I think they must be those which are so white, like pigeons' eggs, in the fall, the thick, leathery rind bursting into eight to eleven segments, like those of a boy's batting ball, and curving back. They are very pretty and remarkable now, sprinkled over the sand, smooth and plump on account of the rain. (I find some beyond at Mountain Sumach Knoll, smaller with a very thin rind and more turned back, a different species plainly.) The inside of the rind, which is uppermost, approaches a chocolate-color; the puffball is a rough dirty or brownish white; the dust which does not fly now at any rate is chocolate-colored. Seeing these thus open, I should know there had been wet weather.

The star fungi, as they dried in my chamber in the course of two or three hours, drew in the fingers. The different segments curled back tightly upon the central puff, the points being strongly curled downward into the middle dimple-wise. It requires wet weather, then, to expand and display them to advantage. They are hygrometers. Their coat seems to be composed of two thicknesses of different material and quality, and I should guess that the inside chocolate-colored had a great affinity for moisture and, being saturated with it, swelled, and so necessarily burst off and turned back, and perchance the outside dirty-white or pale-brown one expands with dryness. —April 22, 1856

EARTHSTARS ARE MOST PICTURESQUE. WHEN YOUNG THE PLANTS are sunk deep in the soil, connected to it by an abundance of mycelium. The thick and leathery outer coat of this puffball completely covers the inner ball or puffball proper. At maturity, they emerge from ground and the outer coat breaks its connection with the mycelium and splits apart into several reflexed rays that lift the still-attached inner spore case into the air. There it sits upon the ground, a papery ball with an apical mouth, surrounded by the leathery star.

The Smallest Earthstar
Scleroderma minimus

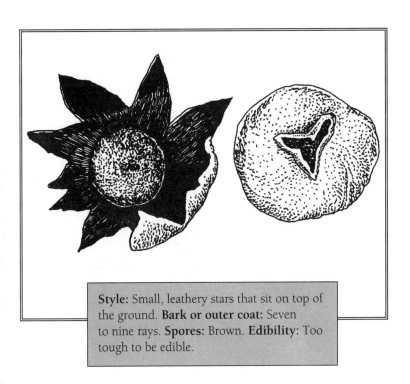

Style: Small, leathery stars that sit on top of the ground. **Bark or outer coat:** Seven to nine rays. **Spores:** Brown. **Edibility:** Too tough to be edible.

WHEN OPEN, THE SMALLEST EARTHSTAR HAS SEVEN TO NINE LOBES. THE round center is up to an inch in diameter, white to pale brown, and seated on a plain circular disk. At first it's completely below ground but then pushes its way up through mostly sandy soils from August through November throughout North America. *Geastrum floriforme,* another pretty earthstar, is about an inch across. It appears singly or in small groups on sandy soil throughout North America.

The Water-Measuring Earthstar
Astraeus hygrometricus

Style: Deeply parted rays that are strongly hygrometric, expanding to a breadth of two to three inches. **Bark or outer coat:** Seven to twenty rays. **Spores:** Brown. **Edibility:** Too tough to be edible.

[John Russell] says that my five-fingered fungus is the Lycoperdon stellatum *and can be found now. I find it in some places. (It is different from the white rough-coated puffball now found.) It was exhibited lately in Boston as the "resurrection plant"(!!) to compete with the one imported from Palestine.* —July 1856

HAVING FOUND NO REFERENCE TO *LYCOPERDON STELLATUM,* I ASSUME THAT this was another scientific name for *Astraeus hygrometricus.*

Nina Marshall, in *The Mushroom Book,* describes the resurgent qualities of the water-measuring earthstar: "When the weather is wet, the lining of the points of the star become gelatinous and lie flat on the ground, anchoring the plant firmly; but when the weather is dry, the soft, gelatinous part becomes hard and rigid, and curls the segments up around the inner ball; then the wind rolls it about, and it scatters its spores from the hole in the apex of the ball as it rolls. It is a fair-weather traveler, always resting at night and on damp days."

Like the pale white Indian pipes, all the previous plants are oddities, but imagine the garden you would have if the path to the strawberry patch were lined by neat columns of giant puffballs or the winter rock garden could be festooned with dozens of earthstars, each one looking like an overbaked sugar cookie, a solid shape on the melting snows of early spring.

THE EVENING PRIMROSE
Oenothera biennis

Style: Flowers are dull and forlorn by day but bright and flamboyant at night, blooming on plants that can reach five feet. **Leaves:** Four to eight inches long, slightly toothed and lanceolate. **Flowers:** Lemon yellow four-petaled blossoms up to two inches wide open in late afternoon to evening. **Fruit:** An oblong capsule about an inch and a half long. **Zone:** 5. **Uses:** Great for the wild or meadow garden and the back of the border or as a specimen plant for educational purposes. **Culture:** Full sun to partial shade in well-drained but average soil.

The tree-primrose (scabish) (Oenothera biennis), a rather coarse yellow flower with a long tubular calyx, naturalized extensively in Europe. Jacob Bigelow, in his Florula Bostoniensis, *says of this plant, now generally called the evening-primrose, "In the country it is vulgarly known by the name of Scabish, a corruption probably of Scabious, from which however it is a very different plant."* —June 29, 1851

The *Oxford English Dictionary* does indeed equate scabish with the evening primrose. The entry refers to the word as a corruption of scabious, and traces the mistake to one Mrs. Lincoln, who used the term—I hope, much to the dismay of those in attendance—while lecturing between 1845 and 1850. Scabious is a blanket term for the various herbs used to treat scabies, the scab, the mange, and the itch.

The genus name *Oenothera* is from the Greek words *onios*, wine, and *thera*, to hunt. When first named, these plants were confused with another genus that had roots bearing the aroma of wine. The species name refers to their biennial nature. In addition to evening primrose, the plants are also called night willow-herb. They are distributed from Labrador to the Gulf of Mexico, west to the Rocky Mountains, and on to the West Coast.

The evening primrose was one of the first American species introduced to England and Europe and as far as I can tell, it made the journey as early as 1614. Most plants journeyed the other way, either loaded with seeds brought over to our shores in the earthen ballast of ships that carried cargo back to crown and country or packed up with the settlers' baggage. In England the plant was called the sundrop (a misnomer—sundrops are day-blooming primroses) and the tree primrose.

In both England and Germany, the roots were used as food and the young shoots for salads. Peeled and simmered in two changes of salted water, the roots are supposed to be a fine-tasting vegetable. By a strange twist of fate, the plant was reintroduced to American gardeners as German rampion.

But these plants were imported not only for their edible qualities but for their medicinal uses too. *Potter's New Cyclopedia of Medicinal Herbs and Preparations* (New York: Harper & Row, 1972), a book that first appeared back in 1907, notes that one Professor Scudder employed the plant with success in the treatment of functional gastrointestinal disorders. American Indians brewed a root tea to treat obesity and bowel pains and made a root poultice for doctoring piles and bruises, besides rubbing the root on muscles (sometimes mixed with deer fat) to give athletes extra strength. Recent research from the pharmaceutical industry points to its possible use in helping atopic eczema, allergy-induced eczema, asthma, migraines, premenstrual syndrome, various inflammations, metabolic disorders, diabetes, arthritis, and alcoholism. Is it surprising that somebody tried it on scabies? Evening primrose oil is a natural source of essential fatty acids like gamma-linolenic acid, and various preparations are found in every health food store.

The large evening primrose below the foot of our garden does not open till some time between 6:30 and 8:00 P.M. or sundown. It was not open when I went to bathe, but freshly out in the cool of the evening at sundown, as if enjoying the serenity of the hour.   —*July 5, 1856*

Twilight in Thoreau's Garden is a wonderful time. Between the open glow of dusk and the pitch black of impending night, there is a short period on summer evenings—ten to fifteen minutes at best—when the atmosphere takes on a luminous quality, magnifying the yellow of the primrose petal; that is the time when this plant is at its best.

In August, Thoreau again watched the plants bloom:

Saw the primrose open at sundown. The corolla burst part
way open and unfolded rapidly; the sepals flew back with a
smart spring. In a minute or two the corolla was opened flat and
seemed to rejoice in the cool, serene light and air.

—*August 12, 1856*

Many writers of the nineteenth and early twentieth centuries remarked on the quick opening of the flowers, and some, like Alice Morse Earle, reported that upon opening, the blossoms made a distinct sound. Mrs. Margaret Deland, an American novelist and poet, described the flower in *Old Garden:*

> There the primrose stands, that as the night
> Begins to gather, and the dews to fall,
> Flings wide to circling moths her twisted buds,
> That shine like yellow moons with pale cold glow,
> And all the air her heavy fragrance floods,
> And gives largess to any winds that blow.
> Here in warm darkness of a night in June,
> . . . children came
> To watch the primrose blow. Silently they stood
> Hand clasped in hand, in breathless hush around,
> And saw her slyly doff her soft green hood
> And blossom—with a silken burst of sound.

The flower petals are held together by tiny hooks at their tips. As the pressure of sap forces the petals to expand, they part at the bottom but remain fixed at the top until, finally, the hooks snap apart; the corolla opens up almost instantaneously, then slows as the petals spread out flat, the whole process taking about thirty minutes for each flower. I've never been able to hear a sound connected with the process, but it's nice to think that someone once thought she did.

The fragrance of these flowers is barely discernible by day but toward evening it becomes increasingly powerful. Why? Because at twilight the sphinx moths, and some smaller moths, too, fly to the flowers, answering the scented lure of these moth-pollinated flowers. As they hover over the blossoms, their long tongues can easily reach to the bottom of the floral tube and drain the last drops of the nectar hidden there. Sticky pollen hangs from the various flower parts and is easily picked up by the moths and carried to nearby blossoms. If a flower is not pollinated by night, it will remain open for a few hours in the early morning—or on cloudy days—ready to receive a bumblebee or sometimes a hummingbird to complete its fertilization.

Because it is a biennial, the first year sees the growth of a rosette of leaves; flowering takes place during the following summer. The plants drop seed easily and new plants appear at the base of the parent plant, germinating that first summer and guaranteeing flowers for next year.

And speaking of germination, *Oenothera biennis* seed was subjected to the same experiment in which pokeweed seeds were buried for years to see how long they would remain viable. After seventy years of burial in sealed containers, these seeds would still germinate.

A new cultivar of this plant called 'Tina James' Magic Primrose' bears flowers two inches across and blooms for six weeks or more. Now called *Oenothera glaziovinia,* the species is another name for *O. erythrosepala,* once called *O. lamarckiana* but really a cultivar.

One final note on the common evening primrose. In 1901 the Dutch botanist Hugo de Vries published his monumental study *Die Mutationstheorie,* in which he formulated the idea that evolution occurs through sudden, large mutations rather than through a series of gradual changes. His results were based on a wide knowledge of plant behavior, but most of his observations were made of a species of evening primrose growing in his backyard. *Oenothera lamarckiana* was originally named for Jean Baptiste Lamarck, the French naturalist who lost out to Darwin in the evolutionary sweepstakes.

De Vries found his first clump of this evening primrose in an abandoned "waste place" at Hilversum in Holland and noticed that in addition to the normal plants, two obvious variations were present. He dug up all three and took them home to his garden, where he studied these and other mutations. Because the variations bred true generation after generation, he thought the plants were new species—although today they would probably be called cultivars.

During his work on evening primroses, de Vries chanced upon Mendel's laws of heredity. These observations based on garden peas had been lost for decades. In his writings de Vries gave Mendel full credit.

Although all this activity took place in Europe, remember that the evening primroses are American plants.

THE SUNDROPS
Oenothera fruticosa and O. perennis

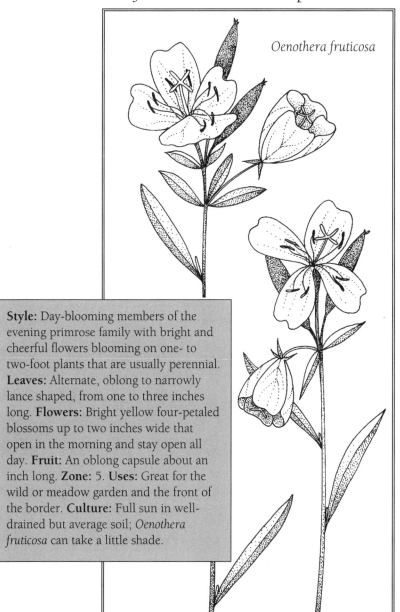

Oenothera fruticosa

Style: Day-blooming members of the evening primrose family with bright and cheerful flowers blooming on one- to two-foot plants that are usually perennial. **Leaves:** Alternate, oblong to narrowly lance shaped, from one to three inches long. **Flowers:** Bright yellow four-petaled blossoms up to two inches wide that open in the morning and stay open all day. **Fruit:** An oblong capsule about an inch long. **Zone:** 5. **Uses:** Great for the wild or meadow garden and the front of the border. **Culture:** Full sun in well-drained but average soil; *Oenothera fruticosa* can take a little shade.

The Oenothera pumila, *or dwarf tree-primrose, a neat yellow flower, abounds in the meadows; which the careless would mistake at a distance for buttercups.*   —June 30, 1851

*O*enothera pumila is really *O. perennis,* a member of the day-flowering species in this genus and known by the common name of sundrops. These thin, one-stemmed plants bear a cluster of bright yellow flowers that rival the sun in their intensity. The flowers hang down before they open from stems that bear minute glands. The petals are heart shaped, up to a third of an inch long, and have noticeable veining. Because this species usually grows no higher than twenty inches, it's a perfect plant for small gardens or the edges of a wildflower collection.

Oenothera fruticosa is the more common sundrops of the garden. It is distinguished by the long, tapering stalklike appendage at the base of the seedpod and variably shaped leaves. Some plants may reach three feet. This species is an aggressive spreader but because it's shallow rooted, unwanted plants are easily pulled out.

The flowers of both species are pollinated by bumblebees, and sometimes by butterflies, chiefly the common white cabbage butterfly *(Pieris rapae).* Even though the smaller insects cannot reach the nectar, they flock to the abundant pollen.

Sundrops' promiscuous sex life results in a bewildering number of hybrids, so don't be surprised if you find minor variations among plants. They make up for this habit in the way they withstand dry soil, stand up to summer sun, and brightly confront a clear blue sky.

BALM-OF-GILEAD
Populus x gileadensis

Style: A large tree of unknown origin found along roadsides and in old fields. The very large red buds of this tree are varnished with an abundance of sticky, fragrant resin. **Leaves:** More or less heart shaped and up to six inches long, with hairy stems and lower surfaces. **Flowers:** Long, drooping catkins. **Fruit:** A small capsule containing seeds surrounded with copius hairs. **Zone:** 2. **Uses:** Grown in gardens and on farms for the sap produced by the buds. Quick growing and useful as a screen. **Culture:** Tolerant of most conditions but does best in a light sandy soil in full sun.

The buds of the balm-of-Gilead [are] coated with a gummy substance, mahogany-colored, [and] already have a fragrant odor. . . . The aments [or catkins] . . . are just beginning to appear and they are female, with the large leaf-bud in the centre. The leaves in the last are larger and more developed than those of any tree which I have noticed this season. The bud is filled with a fragrant, viscid balsam, which is yellowish and difficult to wash from the fingers. It is an agreeable fragrance at this season. —April 26, 1852

How aromatic the balm-of-Gilead buds now! —May 1, 1853

The rain is over. There is a bow in the east. The earth is refreshed; the grass is wet. The air is warm again and still. The rain has soothed the water to a glassy smoothness. It is very beautiful on the water now. . . . Ground ivy just begins to leaf. I am surprised to find the great poplar at the Island conspicuously in leaf,—leaves more than an inch broad, from top to bottom of the tree, and are already fluttering in the wind,—and others near it—conspicuously before any other native tree, as tenderly green, wet, and glossy as if this shower had opened them. . . . The balm-of-Gilead is rapidly expanding, and I scent it in the twilight twenty rods off. —May 11, 1854

The origins of few American trees are shrouded in mystery but the franklinia and balm-of-Gilead spring to mind. Although it can survive in USDA Zone 6, the franklinia is usually considered a southern tree, and Thoreau never wrote about it. Originally named *Gordonia alatamaha* (a genus that includes some thirty trees of Asia and the American Southeast), the tree is now in its own genus, *Franklinia*. It was discovered in a small area on the Altamaha River in Georgia by John and William Bartram, supposedly in 1765. In 1773, William returned to the spot to collect seeds and went back once or twice more for plants and seeds, introducing the tree to both Philadelphia and England. In 1790, Dr. Moses Marshall found the tree again in the same place that the Bartrams had found it. Since that time the franklinia has never again been seen in the wild and its disappearance has never been explained. Thankfully, it's now in cultivation in America and Europe.

Thoreau did write about the balm-of-Gilead, and like the franklinia, its origins are also mysterious. The scientific name is *Populus* x *gileadensis,* because this tree is presumed to be a hybrid between *P. balsamifera,* the balsam poplar or hackmatack tree, and *P. deltoides,* the cottonwood. Some authorities claim it is a clone of *P. balsamifera* var. *subcordata,* a balsam poplar with a different leaf shape than the type. A few books call it *P. candicans* and note that it might originally be from Asia. But nobody is sure.

And I'm not sure that the tree Thoreau called the balm-of-Gilead was not in reality *Populus balsamifera.* He was too inexact in his journal description to confirm it one way or the other.

Only sterile female trees are known, so the tree can be propagated only by digging up suckers or by taking cuttings. One way or another the balm-of-Gilead now grows in North Carolina along the Pigeon River in Haywood County, on into the Smokies, up through the Appalachians, and into New York's Catskill Mountains.

The first mention of the balm-of-Gilead (a land east of Jordan) is in the Bible (Genesis 43:11), when Israel advised Judah to take both presents and money to Joseph in Egypt and include "a little balm and a little honey."

The biblical balm-of-Gilead was *Commiphora opobalsamum,* or Mecca balsam, a tree that produced an agreeable resin highly prized in the East as an unguent and cosmetic. The balm came in three forms: xylobalsamum, obtained by steeping the new twigs; carpobalsamum, pressed from the fruit; and opobalsamum, extracted from the kernel of the fruit. At one time it was believed that if a person coated a finger with the balm, he or she could pass it through fire without ill effect. Hence the phrase "there is balm in Gilead" was used to comfort the ill and afflicted.

Thoreau also mentions the balsam fir *(Abies balsamea):*

> *I first observed about ten days ago that the fresh shoots of the fir balsam, found under the tree wilted, or plucked and kept in the pocket or in the house a few days, emit the fragrance of strawberries, only it is somewhat more aromatic and spicy. It was to me a very remarkable fragrance to be emitted by a pine. A very rich, delicious, aromatic, spicy fragrance, which if the fresh and living shoots emitted, they would be still more to be sought after.*   —*June 30, 1851*

Though Thoreau never called this fir the balm-of-Gilead, others did. Writing in *The Fragrant Path* (New York: The Macmillan Company, 1932), Louise Beebe Wilder quoted Thoreau about shoots "kept in the pocket" but referred to the balsam fir as the balm-of-Gilead.

In *The Tree Book* (New York: Doubleday, Page & Company, 1914), Julia Ellen Rogers refers to *Populus balsamifera* as the balm-of-Gilead. The author describes great forests of this poplar stretching away to the margins of the Great Lakes and the bottom lands of upper Canada, calling them the "most prominent feature of vegetation in the vast regions that approach the Arctic circle, and extend down into the northern tier of states, from ocean to ocean."

The large tree she describes reaches a height of sixty to eighty feet and also goes by the names of hairy balm-of-Gilead, hackmatack, balm buds, black poplar, and cottonwood.

The Indians of North America called *Populus balsamifera* the tacamahac. They extracted fragrant waxes from winter buds to seal up the seams of birchbark canoes. Not long after honeybees arrived from Europe and England, they were spotted using tacamahac wax to seal up weather cracks in their hives. The material is known to beekeepers as propolis, a word that covers a number of resinous tree exudations that bees collect to patch leaks and to cover any roughness within the hive.

The Indians were also well acquainted with the medicinal properties of this poplar. By boiling the resinous buds in various animal fats, they made a salve for dressing wounds, sores, and eczema. This ointment was also rubbed on the nostrils to relieve colds and flu because the turpentinelike odor helped to open clogged respiratory passages. Early settlers used the fragrant resin as an ingredient in cough medicines, and a liniment made by macerating the buds in oil was used in the treatment of rheumatism.

THE BLACK-EYED SUSAN AND OTHER CONEFLOWERS
Rudbeckia spp.

Rudbeckia hirta

Style: Annual, biennial, or short-lived perennial; a tough but charming wildflower of open fields and meadows on one- to two-foot stems. **Leaves:** Lanceolate, narrow, and rough to the touch; the lower leaves on stems and the upper leaves sessile. **Flowers:** Large and solitary, composed of both ray and disk flowers: the former bright orange-yellow, almost two inches long; the latter cone shaped and chocolate brown. **Zone:** 4. **Uses:** Great for the wild or meadow garden. **Culture:** Full sun in average well-drained garden soil; drought resistant.

What a luxury to bathe now! It is gloriously hot,—the first of this weather. I cannot get wet enough. I must let the water soak into me. When you come out, it is rapidly dried on you or absorbed into your body, and you want to go in again. I begin to inhabit the planet, and see how I may be naturalized at last. The clams are so thick on the bottom at Hubbard's Bathing Place that standing up to my neck in water, I brought my feet together and lifted up between them, so as to take of in my hand without dipping my head, three clams the first time, though many more dropped off. When you consider the difficulty of carrying two melons under an arm and that this was in the water, you may infer the number of the clams.

A cone-flower (new plant), Rudbeckia hirta (except that I call its disk not dull brown but dull or dark purple or maroon; however Wood calls it dark purple),—in Arethusa Meadow. Saw one plucked June 25; blossomed probably about that time. Many yesterday in meadows behind almshouse. Probably introduced lately from West.   *—July 2, 1854*

Originally classified by the father of modern botanical nomenclature, Linnaeus, the genus *Rudbeckia* is named in honor of Olaf Rudbeck and his son, who were both botany professors at Uppsala University in Sweden.

Concerning the origin of the plants, Thoreau was right. These field flowers did come from the West. "So very many weeds having come to our Eastern shores from Europe," wrote Neltje Blanchan, "and marched farther and farther west year by year, it is but fair that black-eyed Susan, a native of Western clover fields, should travel toward the Atlantic in bundles of hay whenever she gets the chance, to repay Eastern farmers in their own coin. Do these gorgeous heads know that all our showy rudbeckias—some with orange red at the base of their ray florets—have become prime favorites of late years in European gardens, so offering them still another chance to overrun the Old World, to which so much American hay is shipped."

Rudbeckias begin to bloom in July and will continue until cut down by frost. All are short-lived perennials except the black-eyed Susan, which depends on a number of unknowns to guarantee its roots lasting over the winter. But the plants will self-seed with such vigor that they can, on occasion, become almost weeds. Seeds sown early in spring will produce flowering plants the first year, so in the garden these flowers can be treated as annuals.

Rudbeckias have an amazing resistance to drought, and even badly wilted plants will quickly perk up with a bit of water. Thus they are most valuable plants where summers are dry. Any soil is acceptable, but they will bloom with more exuberance when given a bit of manure or plant food. It's best to move plants in spring when the first leaves—easily recognized since they are oval and covered with soft, silvery hairs—push up through the soil, but with enough water, all except the black-eyed Susan can be shifted about the garden even in July. Whiteflies have a penchant for these wild-flowers, but they do not seem to bother the plants to any extent.

In the last decade the popularity of the coneflowers has grown especially since they combine so beautifully with the many popular ornamental grasses. In fact, the combination of coneflowers and variegated maiden grass (*Miscanthus sinensis* 'Variegatus') has become almost a garden cliché.

Dr. A. F. Blankeslee is credited with developing the gloriosa daisy. From the original black-eyed Susan, he developed hybrids with blossoms that are often seven inches wide in varying shades of orange, yellow, gold, tan, brown, and dark red.

'Irish Eyes' has a green eye instead of black and 'Goldilocks' has double golden yellow flowers on fifteen-inch stems.

The root of *Rudbeckia hirta* has been used by the American Indians to brew a tea for treating colds, earaches, and snakebite.

Those with sensitive skin should be warned that some people get dermatitis from handling the leaves and stems.

Rudbeckia fulgida, or the orange coneflower, journeyed north from the South. It's usually offered as the cultivar 'Goldsturm', a magnificent plant with thirty-inch stems bearing dozens of three- to four-inch flowers that bloom throughout the summer into fall.

First described in 1753, *Rudbeckia laciniata* is a native coneflower often reaching a height of ten feet in the wild. It's not particularly attractive in the garden, but around old farmhouses and in abandoned gardens the double-flowered cultivar 'Golden Glow' still survives, having been in cultivation since before 1913. This cultivar often grows to seven feet and usually needs staking, but placed to the rear of a wild garden it has great color and charm. A newer cultivar (introduced in 1951), known as 'Goldquelle', seldom tops thirty inches and is not invasive.

The blossoms of *Rudbeckia triloba,* brown-eyed Susan, have golden yellow rays encircling brown centers. The two-inch flowers top four-foot stems. They are native from southern New England to Minnesota and south to Georgia and Oklahoma. Listed as both biennial and perennial, they self-sow with ease and are excellent for naturalizing in the wild garden or at the edge of a meadow.

There's a field in Thoreau's Garden that rises up a slope that's decidedly stony. Over the next few years, I hope the black-eyed Susans thrive and dot those waving grasses with their sparkling yellow.

THE PRAIRIE GRASSES
IN THE GREAT MEADOWS

*Two interesting tall purplish grasses, appear to be the prevailing ones now in dry and sterile neglected fields and hillsides,—*Andropogon furcatus, *forked beard grass, and apparently* Andropogon scoparius, *purple wood grass, though the last appears to have three awns like an* Aristida. *The first is a very tall and slender-culmed grass, with four or five purple finger-like spikes, raying upward from the top. It is very abundant on the hillside behind Peter's. The other is quite slender, two to three or four feet high, growing in tufts and somewhat curving, also commonly purple and with pretty purple stigmas like the last, and it has purple anthers. When out of bloom, its appressed spikes are recurving and have a whitish hairy or fuzzy look. These are the prevailing conspicuous flowers where I walk this afternoon in dry ground. I have sympathy with them because they are despised by the farmer and occupy sterile and neglected soil. They also by their rich purple reflections or tinges seem to express the ripeness of the year. It is high-colored like ripe grapes, and expresses a maturity which the spring did not suggest. Only the August sun could have thus burnished these culms and leaves. The farmer has long since done his upland haying, and he will not deign to bring his scythe to where these slender wild grasses have at length flowered thinly. You often see the bare sand between them. I walk encouraged between the tufts of purple wood grass, over the sandy fields by the shrub oaks, glad to recognize these simple contemporaries. These two are almost the first grasses that I have learned to distinguish. I did not know by how many friends I was surrounded. The purple of their culms excites me like that of the pokeweed stems.* —August 26, 1858

Thoreau obviously enjoyed the natural world around him and in this he had few peers. He knew that his views rarely coincided with the contemporary power elite of New England. When

Thoreau wrote that he was happier in the field than in the city, he meant it.

> *Think what refuge there is for me before August is over, from college commencements and society that isolates me! I can skulk amid the tufts of purple wood grass on the borders of the Great Fields! Wherever I walk this afternoon the purple-fingered grass stands like a guide-board and points my thoughts to more poetic paths than they have lately traveled.*
> —*August 26, 1858*

The two grasses that Thoreau described are known today as the bluestems, little and big. Both grasses are found over most of the United States, but big bluestem was one of the principal grasses of the tall-grass prairie that spawned the rich black soils of today's corn belt. Very little original prairie still exists, but big bluestem is still found on untilled prairie land.

Little Bluestem Grass
Schizachyrium (Andropogon) scoparium

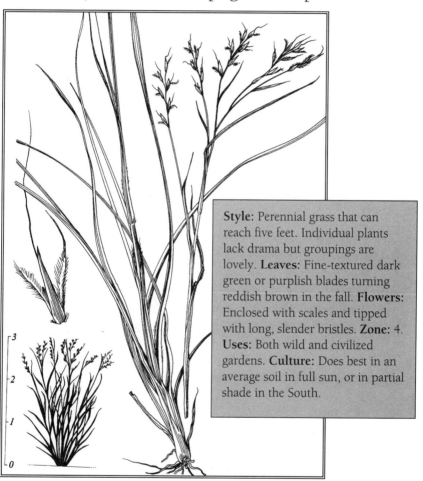

Style: Perennial grass that can reach five feet. Individual plants lack drama but groupings are lovely. **Leaves:** Fine-textured dark green or purplish blades turning reddish brown in the fall. **Flowers:** Enclosed with scales and tipped with long, slender bristles. **Zone:** 4. **Uses:** Both wild and civilized gardens. **Culture:** Does best in an average soil in full sun, or in partial shade in the South.

THOREAU CALLED LITTLE BLUESTEM GRASS BY THE NAME PURPLE WOOD grass. His was the better name. Little bluestem is a description that fits the plant well in early spring, when the new stems have a bluish cast, but is meaningless for the rest of the year, especially after late summer when the plant turns a golden tan. Other common names include broom grass, broom beard grass, wiregrass, bunchgrass, prairie bluegrass, and broom. Plants occur over most of the United States, but characteristically it's a grass of dry prairies, plains, rocky slopes, and open woods. Bluestem provides forage in the Midwest and the West, especially for cattle and horses. In fact, during the 1930s, the Civilian Conservation Corps planted bluestem to control erosion.

In 1803, the French botanist André Michaux gave little bluestem the scientific name of *Schizachyrium scoparium,* the genus name referring to the deeply cleft flowering spikes. But in 1903, bluestem was renamed *Andropogon, aner* meaning man, and *pogon,* beard, referring to the silky hairs on the spike. Today, according to the rule of preeminence in botanical nomenclature, the first name given a plant applies, and so *Schizachyrium* is now the correct choice. The species name *scoparium* means "in the form of a broom," again referring to the bristled flowers.

When it comes to describing grass flowers, each flower spike is made up of subdivisions called spikelets, and each spikelet contains parts essentially the same as those of other flowering plants, except that grasses, being pollinated by the wind, not insects, have tiny, vestigial petals. The stigma is usually plumed to aid in picking pollen out of the air, and stamens are very large and flexible to get the pollen out on the breeze.

Grass seeds assume many sizes and shapes, all readily adapted to dispersal by animals, including people, but more often by the wind. Many of the brome grasses have barbed tips that easily penetrate the fur of animals or the clothes of man. Awns (a feature of grasses consisting of a bristlelike spike) often can, with changes in humidity, spiral up and down, screwing their sharp tips directly into an animal's skin. Other grass seeds are less aggressive, instead exhibiting long and attractive plumes that float the seed through the air just like dandelion fluff.

The tufts of Andropogon scoparius, *which is common on the sandy shore under Ball's Hill, and yet more on the hill just behind Reuben Brown's place, are now in their autumnal state,—recurved culms adorned with white fuzzy spikes. The culms still of a dull-red color, quite agreeable in the sun.*

Paddling slowly back, we enjoy at length very perfect reflections in the still water. The blue of the sky, and indeed all tints, are deepened in the reflection.

On Money-Digger's Hill-side, the Andropogon scoparius *now stands in tufts two feet high by one wide, with little whitish plumes along the upper half of its reddish fawn-colored culms. Now in low grounds the different species of bidens or beggar's-ticks adhere to your clothes. These bidents, tridents, quadridents are shot into you by myriads of unnoticed foes.* —October 14, 1858

In November, Thoreau wrote about the transformation in little bluestem.

A true November seat is amid the pretty white-plumed An-dropogon scoparius, the withered culms of the purple wood grass which covers so many dry knolls. There is a large patch at the entrance to Pleasant Meadow. It springs from pink-brown clumps of radical leaves, which make good seats. Looking toward the sun, as I sit in the midst of it rising as high as my head, its countless silvery plumes are a very cheerful sight. At a distance they look like frost on the plant.

When we emerged from the pleasant footpath through the birches into Witherell Glade, looking along it toward the westering sun, the glittering white tufts of the Andropogon scoparius, *lit up by the sun, were affectingly fair and cheering to behold.*   —*November 9, 1858*

The following year in November, the little bluestem is again a featured entry in the journal.

It was already a cheerful Novemberish scene. A narrow glade stretching east and west between a dense birch wood, now half bare, and a ruddy oak wood on the upper side, a ground covered with tawny stubble and fine withered grass and cistuses. Looking eastward along it, your eye fell on these lit tufts of andropogon, their glowing half raised a foot or more above the ground, a lighter and more brilliant whiteness than the downiest cloud presents (though seen on one side they are grayish).

The tufts of purplish withered andropogon in Witherell Glade are still as fair as ever, soft and trembling and bending from the wind; of a very light mouse-color seen from the side of the sun, and as delicate as the most fragile ornaments of a lady's bonnet; but looking toward the sun they are a brilliant white, each polished hair reflecting the November sun without its heats, not in the least yellowish or brown like the goldenrods and asters.   —*November 8, 1859*

Big Bluestem Grass
Andropogon gerardii

Style: Perennial tufted grass that can reach seven feet. **Leaves:** Dark green or purplish blades turning reddish brown in the fall; the foliage is sometimes hairy. **Flowers:** Spikelets in panicles consisting of mostly three to six usually purplish racemes; the dried panicles are very effective in dried flower arrangements. **Zone:** 4. **Uses:** Grown in both wild and civilized gardens. **Culture:** Tolerant of most conditions but does best in an average soil in full sun, although in the South, plants will do well in partial shade. Makes a great windbreak.

THOREAU CALLS THE BIG BLUESTEM (*ANDROPOGON GERARDII*) *A. FURCATUS*, or forked beard grass, sometimes known as turkey grass. It's one of America's great prairie grasses, robust enough to make a specimen plant in a formal garden but doubly effective when used as a background planting or massed in a wild garden or a naturalized area. Like little bluestem, big bluestem is an important forage crop, and still provides a goodly amount of wild hay in the native prairies. This grass turns a beautiful shade of light reddish brown after the first frost and persists in the landscape all winter long. It likes water and is less luxuriant when grown on poor and dry soil. Be patient with these grasses for the first year or two, during which time most of the plant's energies are being spent in sending roots down as deep as ten feet. The deep root system protected the plants from destruction in cyclical droughts and great prairie fires.

Indian Grass
Sorghastrum avenaceum (S. nutans)

Style: Perennial tufted grass that can reach five feet. The attractive flowers are especially welcome because they bloom in the fall. **Leaves:** Medium green leaf blades are narrow and flat, turning orange brown in the fall. **Flowers:** Spikelets with long awns, in bronzy yellow panicles. **Zone:** 4. **Uses:** Grown in both wild and civilized gardens. **Culture:** Tolerant of most conditions but does best in an average soil in full sun, although in the South, plants will do well in partial shade.

On the hillside above Clamshell Ditch, grows that handsome grass of September, evidently Sorghum nutans (Andropogon of Bigelow), chestnut beard grass, Indian grass, wood grass. It is much larger than what I saw before; is still abundantly in flower; four and a half feet high; leaves, perhaps arundinaceous, eighteen inches long; panicle, nine inches long. It is a very handsome, wild-looking grass, well enough called Indian grass, and I should have named it with the other andropogons. With its narrow one-sided panicle of bright purple and yellow (I include the yellow anthers) often waving, raised high above the leaves, it looks like a narrow banner. It is of more vivid colors that its congeners, and might well have caught an Indian's eye. These bright banners are now advanced on the distant hillsides, not in large armies, but scattered troops or single file, like the red men themselves. They stand thus fair and bright in our midst, as it were representative of the race which they are named after, but for the most part unobserved. It stands like an Indian chief taking a last look at his beloved hunting grounds. The expression of this grass haunted me for a week after I first passed and noticed it, like the glance of an eye.

—September 5, 1858

THIS IS THE THIRD OF THE THREE GREAT PRAIRIE GRASSES. IT DOES WELL in almost any condition and, like the bluestems, matures late in the season. The spikelets bear bright yellow anthers loaded with pollen, turning golden brown after the autumn frosts. When frost hits, the foliage turns bright orange. Indian grass is an important component of wild prairie hay. When planted in rows, it makes a great screen. The name *Sorghastrum* means "like sorghum" and indicates that the flowers of these two grasses are very similar in appearance. The species name includes the word *avena*, or oats, and again points to a resemblance between these two grasses.

Each humblest plant, or weed, as we call it, stands there to express some thought or mood of ours, and yet how long it stands in vain! I have walked these Great Fields so many Augusts and never yet distinctly recognized these purple companions that I have there. I have brushed against them and trampled them down . . . and now at last they have . . . risen up and blessed me. Beauty and true wealth are always thus cheap and despised. Heaven, or paradise, might be defined as the place which men avoid.   —*August 8, 1858*

THE GOLDENRODS
Solidago spp.

Solidago odora

Style: Usually tall weedy plants of the open field and meadow, topped with large sprays, disks, or plumes of tiny golden yellow flowers, blooming in fall. Goldenrods hybridize in the wild, making identification difficult. If you spot a particularly attractive specimen in a nearby field and the owner has no objection, move it to your own garden. **Leaves:** Alternate, simple, and entire or toothed. **Flowers:** Composites, like daisies, with both disk and ray flowers. **Zone:** 4. **Uses:** Massing in the wild garden; some of the tamer species fit within the perennial border, and the new cultivars definitely belong there. **Culture:** Goldenrods like plenty of sun and do well even in poor soil.

Already the goldenrod, apparently Solidago stricta, *willow-leaved goldenrod, preaches of the lapse of time, on the Walden road. How many a tale its yellow tells!*

—July 13, 1852

Many a dry field now, like that of Sted Buttrick's on the Great Fields, is one dense mass of the bright-golden recurved wands of the Solidago nemoralis . . . *waving in the wind and turning upward to the light hundreds, if not a thousand, flowerets each. It is the greatest mass of conspicuous flowers in the year, and uniformly from one to two feet high, just rising above the withered grass all over the largest fields, now when pumpkins and other yellow fruits begin to gleam, now before the woods are noticeably changed.*   *—September 11, 1859*

The four-foot-tall early goldenrod, *Solidago nemoralis* (the species name means "pertaining to woods and groves"), looks more like a plumed feather waving in the wind than a flower. Because of the plant's genetic heritage, there are many variations in the form of the flowering sprays, some arching out whereas in others, the effect is of many narrow branches pulled together. This goldenrod is found in dry and open places, or at the edge of fields, from Quebec to North Dakota and south to Florida and Arizona. Although Thoreau mentions *S. stricta* as blooming first, it's usually *S. nemoralis* that beats the rest of the species to flowering. *Solidago* is from the Latin *solidare*, to make whole, from the plant's supposed healing qualities. The common name of goldenrod goes back centuries and after you see a field full of these blooming plants, no other name is quite as good.

The Solidago stricta *begins to yellow the Great Fields in front of [Peter's] house, but the* Solidago nemoralis *is hardly out there yet. The sight of the small rough sunflower about*

> a dry ditch bank and hedge advances me at once further
> toward autumn. At the same time I hear a dry, ripe, autum-
> nal chirp of a cricket. It is the next step to the first golden-
> rod. It grows where it escapes the mower, but no doubt, in
> our localities of plants, we do not know where they would
> prefer to grow if unmolested by man, but rather where they
> best escape his vandalism. . . .
>   Butterflies of various colors are now more abundant than
> I have seen them before, especially the small reddish or coppery
> ones. . . . Being constantly in motion and, as they moved,
> opening and closing their wings to preserve their balance,
> they presented a very lifesome scene. Today I see them on
> the early goldenrod (Solidago stricta).   —July 29, 1853

Solidago stricta is a goldenrod with a restrained growth habit
that allows it into the garden (stricta means upright or very
straight). Toward the top of the three- to four-foot wandlike stems
cluster dozens of golden yellow flower heads. In nature, it's found
growing in damp sandy soil from Florida to Texas, and north to
New England.

> The Solidago thyrsoidea was the goldenrod of the mountain-
> top, from the woods quite to the summit. Any other golden-
> rod was comparatively scarce. It was from two inches to two
> feet high. It grew both in small swamps and in the seams of rocks
> everywhere, and was not in its prime.   —August 9, 1860

The large-leaved goldenrod (Solidago macrophylla) is a very
showy species easily identified—as opposed to most goldenrods—
because of the slim leafstalk on all but the uppermost leaves and
the broad, coarsely toothed lower leaves. In Thoreau's day the
species name was thyrsoidea, a Greek word referring to the shape
of the blossoms, which resemble lilacs or butterfly bushes. The
plants are found in moist, cool, and often shaded places from the

Catskills of New York State, east to Massachusetts, and north to Hudson's Bay.

> *B. says that Pursh states that the sweet-scented goldenrod (Solidago odora) "has for some time [i.e., since before 1817] been an article of exportation to China, where it fetches a high price." And yet is known to very few New-Englanders.* —May 29, 1851

> *I find the Solidago odora out by the path to foot of cliffs beyond Hayden's, maybe twenty or thirty rods into woods about the summit level. It is said to have the odor of anise. It is somewhat like sassafras bark. It must be somewhat dried and then bruised.* —August 7, 1853

> *The Solidago odora grows abundantly behind the Minot house in Lincoln. I collected a large bundle of it. Its flower is stale for the most part and imbrowned. It grows in such thick tufts that you can easily gather it.* —August 29, 1853

The anise smell and flavor of the sweet-scented goldenrod made it a popular plant from the moment the first settlers reached the shores of America. The dried young leaves and flowers make an agreeable tea that was very popular among Hessian mercenaries during the American Revolution, and as Thoreau noted above, during the eighteenth century the plant fetched high prices in China. Oliver Perry Medsger writes that this plant is sometimes called Blue Mountain tea, and mentions that it is still being exported to China, making it a minor rural industry. In addition to its use as a pleasant-tasting tea, sweet goldenrod was also used to stimulate digestion, as a mild astringent, and to treat stomach cramps and headaches.

The slender stems of this plant are crowned with panicles of bright yellow flowers, and it makes an attractive garden addition.

In nature, plants are found growing in dry, often sandy soil from Maine and Vermont, south to Florida, and west to Missouri.

In the fall of 1856, Thoreau tabulated the various goldenrod and aster species he knew, keeping a running score on their state of bloom. On September 24, for example, *Solidago stricta* was past; *S. nemoralis,* about done; *S. altissima,* much past its prime; *S. odora,* not seen that week but most likely done; *S. bicolor,* now in its prime; and *S. latifolia,* also in its prime.

Not only are goldenrods perfectly acceptable plants for the perennial bed or border, they also are excellent as cut flowers and very attractive in late fall after the flowers have faded and gone to seed, the gray-brown floral sprays dusted with snow. And they are perfect to naturalize in the wild garden. If tall plants are unwelcome, cut them to about a foot in early summer and they become shorter, bushier plants.

Goldenrod is a native plant that is spoken of as a weed by most Americans, yet English gardeners have taken it to their beds and borders, applying hybridization and a keen eye to produce a number of beautiful and useful cultivars. *Index Hortensis* alone lists thirty cultivars, for most of which *Solidago canadensis* was one of the parents. 'Golden Baby', a compact plant about two feet high, bears upright sprays of golden flowers, blooming the first year from seed started early in the spring; 'Golden Dwarf' (sometimes called 'Goldzwerg', German for gnome or dwarf) has yellow flowers on foot-high stems; 'Cloth of Gold' has golden blossoms on eighteen-inch stems, blooming in late August; 'Crown of Rays' is bright yellow on eighteen-inch stems; 'Golden Mosa' is lemon yellow on thirty-inch stems; and 'Nagshead' is golden yellow on forty-inch stems.

The sun has shone on the earth, and the goldenrod is his
fruit.   —*August 30, 1853*

Thoreau always gave goldenrods complimentary reviews, but the contemporary new media has maligned goldenrod. For years the plants have been blamed for the problems of autumn's hay fever sufferers when the real culprit is ragweed pollen. The rangy and unkempt ragweed, which unfortunately blooms in the same fields and waste places as goldenrod, throws bushels of sinus-irritating pollen to the winds. Ragweed's tiny green flowers are missed by most observers whereas goldenrod's easily spotted spires of bright, yellow orange blossoms get the blame, a case of mistaken identity that continues today. Ragweed has the unusual and lovely name of *Ambrosia,* meaning immortal or divine, a name applied by Linnaeus for an unknown reason.

When examining a plume of goldenrod flowers you will see that the bright yellow flowers with their often heavy smell attract a large number of insects, including wasps, honeybees and bumble-bees, flies, butterflies, and an assortment of smaller bugs.

Thoreau doesn't mention the most common goldenrod, *Solidago canadensis.* This plant grows between one and five feet tall and has a smooth stem at the base, becoming hairy below the inflorescence. The lance-shaped leaves are sharply toothed and each has three conspicuous veins. The flowers, which appear in a broad, triangular panicle, bloom from July to September throughout fields and along roadsides throughout the East.

The American Indians used the roots of this plant for treating burns, made a flower tea for reducing fevers, chewed the fresh flowers for bad sore throats, and made a poultice of the root for snakebites.

> *How richly and exuberantly downy are many goldenrod and aster heads now, their seed just on the point of falling or being blown away, before they are in the least weather-beaten! They are now puffed up to their utmost, clean and light.* —November 8, 1859

The dried stalks of goldenrod make beautiful additions to winter bouquets. Pick the stems when only about one-third of the blossoms are open, and air-dry them by hanging them in a dark but well-ventilated room. The flowers will generally stay in the condition they were in when picked.

> *Saw some green galls on a goldenrod three quarters of an inch in diameter [sketch], shaped like a fruit or an Eastern temple, with two or three little worms inside, completely changing the destiny of the plant, showing the intimate relation between animal and vegetable life. The animal signifies its wishes by a touch, and the plant, instead of going on to blossom and bear its normal fruit, devotes itself to the service of the insect and becomes its cradle and food. It suggests that Nature is a kind of gall, that the Creator stung her and man is the grub she is destined to house and feed. The plant rounds off and paints the gall with as much care and love as its own flower and fruit admiring it perchance even more.*
>
> *—July 30, 1853*

Galls are insect-caused swellings found on hundreds of plant species, ranging from conifers, oaks, and hickories to raspberries and blackberries to many herbaceous plants, including goldenrod. Thoreau mentioned them a number of times and continued to document their occurrence and their forms throughout the journal.

The first-century A.D. Roman naturalist Pliny the Elder believed galls sprang up at night, only to be consumed by flies during the day. In the seventeenth century Francesco Redi, a naturalist and poet, assumed that the plant's vegetable soul produced galls containing eggs, and the eventual insects. Redi was the same man who, using flies and spoiled meat, proved that maggots did not arise by spontaneous generation. Yet he missed with galls. Not until late in the seventeenth century did anyone record that galls were the result of punctures made by insects through which they inject a chemical that causes the swelling; Marcello Malpighi gets the credit.

The gall and the plant have a strange relationship. The plant would be better off without the insect, but once the pest arrives, it's certainly an advantage to seal it off in the prison of the gall. So the insect is the real winner, gaining food and lodging without any real effort.

Eurosta solidaginis, a fruit fly, is the major cause of goldenrod galls.

THE CATTAIL
Typha latifolia

Style: A tall water plant with stout stems that bear spikes. **Leaves:** Erect and blade-like, up to one inch wide and three to nine feet long. **Flowers:** A sausagelike head of tightly packed female flowers, topped with a tail of staminate flowers. **Zone:** 3. **Uses:** For the edge of a pond or lake or in pots for the small pool. **Culture:** Cattails are not fussy, needing only wet soil, fresh meadows, marshes, or a few inches of water at the edge of a pond. **Caution:** Except for the cultivars, cattails are *highly* invasive.

*The still dead-looking willows and button-bushes are alive
with red-wings, now perched on a yielding twig, now pursu-
ing a female swiftly over the meadow, now starting across
the stream. No two have epaulets equally brilliant. Some
are small and almost white, and others a brilliant vermilion.
They are handsomer than the golden robins . . . the rich
colors and the rich and varied notes of the blackbirds surpass
them all.* —May 13, 1853

Current botanical references list ten species of cattails in the
temperate and tropical regions of both hemispheres. The
genus is derived from the Greek *tuphe,* the ancient name of the plant.
The plants are distributed throughout North America, except in
the extreme north, and Eurasia.

In England and Europe, cattails are known as bulrushes, a
name that in America is given to horsetails and sedges.

Thoreau found the cattails fascinating. He marveled at the
amount of material that nature packs into one cattail flower. The
"cat's tail" is made up of thousands of tiny flowers, each little more
than one pistil. Above the "hot dog" is a very slender spike of male
flowers that disappear after their pollen falls.

*We turned down the brook at Heywood's meadow. It was
worth the while to see how the water, even in the marsh
where the brook is almost stagnant, sparkled in this atmosphere, for though warm it is remarkably clear. Water which
in summer would look dark and perhaps turbid now
sparkles like the lakes in November. The water is the more
attractive, since all around is deep snow. The brook here is
full of cattails or reed mace. I found, on pulling open or
breaking in my hand, as one would break bread, the still
nearly perfect spikes of this fine reed, that the flowers were
red or crimson at their base, where united to the stem. When
I rubbed off thus what was at first but a thimbleful of these*

dry flowerets, they suddenly took in air and flushed up like powder, expanding like feathers and foam, filling and over-flowing my hand, to which they imparted a sensation of warmth quite remarkable. I was astonished to see how a small quantity was expanded and inflated on being released and given to the air, and I could not be tired with repeating the experiment. I think a single one would more than fill a half-peck measure if they lay as light as at first in the air. It is something magical to one who tries it for the first time. Like a puff of powder it flashes up. You do not know at first where they all come from. It is the conjurer's trick in nature, equal to taking feathers enough to fill a bed out of a hat. When you had done, but still will scrape the almost bare stem, still they overflow your hand as before. See it again, and try the com-bustibility of the pollen. As the flowerets are opening and liberating themselves, showing their red extremities, it has the effect of a changeable color. —January 25, 1852*

The cattail down puffs and swells in your hand like a mist, or the conjurer's trick of filling a hat with feathers, for when you have rubbed off but a thimbleful, and can close and con-ceal the wound completely, the expanded down fills your hand to overflowing. Apparently there is a spring to the fine elastic threads which compose the down, which, after having been so long closely packed, on being the least relieved at the base, spring open apace into the form of parachutes to con-vey the seed afar. Where birds or the winds or ice have as-saulted them, this has spread like an eruption. Again, when I rub off the down of the spike with my thumb, I am sur-prised at the sensation of warmth it imparts to my hand, as it flushes over it magically, at the same time revealing a faint purplish-crimson tinge at the base of the down, as it rolls off and expands. It is a very pleasing experiment to try.
—March 23, 1853*

Typha latifolia may have shed pollen two or three days. I am surprised at the abundance of its sulphur-like pollen, on the least jar covering my hands and clothes,—green; at least it does not burn. The female part of the spike is green and solid and apparently immature. —June 18, 1854

Above the Sudbury causeway, I notice again that remarkable large and tall typha, apparently T. latifolia. It is seven or eight feet high (its leaves), with leaves flat on one side (only concave at base, the sheathing part) and regularly convex on the other. They are so much taller than any I see elsewhere as to appear a peculiar species. Long out of bloom. They are what you may call the tallest reed of the meadows, unless you rank the arundo with them, but these are hardly so tall. —July 31, 1859

The uses of cattails are many: flour can be made from the pollen; the stems and leaves are excellent for thatching (a dying art) and weaving chair seats; the fluff is a good substitute for kapok; when broken up, the tails make marvelous stuffing for pillows; young flower spikes make a more than passable cooked vegetable; the pollen may be mixed with other flours to impart flavor and better color than artificial dyes; the sprouts at the end of the rootstock can be cooked as a vegetable; the thickened rootstock may be roasted or boiled for food in the wild; the white and tender parts of spring shoots make an excellent substitute for asparagus; and the pollen has occasionally been utilized by fireworks manufacturers because it's flammable.

Another name for the cattail is the Cossack asparagus, because the young, fruiting spikes are said to be edible when roasted. The roots and the lower part of the stem are sometimes used in salads, and when the rind is peeled off young stems, from the root to eighteen inches up the stem, the white, tender result is said to be very good.

The American Indians used cattails to make a jellylike compound to apply to sores, boils, wounds, and even burns. The fuzz from mature female flower heads was also applied to burns, and actually used as a kind of talcum powder to prevent chafing in babies. Young flower heads were ingested to treat diarrhea. A root tea made of the narrow-leaved cattail *(Typha angustifolia)*, the other common cattail in our area, was used to treat kidney stones. The narrow-leaved cattail has a short space of bare stem between the male and female flower clusters.

Wildlife shares with people the food and homemaking uses of the plant. The water birds alone would mourn its loss, because cattails are a fine source of soft lining for nests, not to mention that perch for redwings; and with its passing, the muskrat would lose its favorite comestibles.

Many people gather cattails for dried flower arrangements. According to Barbara Radcliffe Rogers in *The Encyclopedia of Everlastings* (New York: Weidenfeld & Nicolson, 1988), cattails are easy to dry if they are picked at the right stage. Gather them while the male flowers are blooming, then air-dry them in a standing position. If picked too late, the cylinders will release those puffy masses of airborne seeds that Thoreau was so taken with, eventually blowing throughout the house and grounds.

T. latifolia 'Variegata' has vertical green-and-white stripes on its leaves; because the variegations cut back on the food production of the leaf, this cultivar is less invasive than the species. The two-foot-tall miniature cattail, *Typha minima,* bears very narrow leaves and very small blossoms; its flower heads look more like Vienna sausages than hot dogs.

THE HEMLOCKS
Tsuga spp.

Tsuga canadensis

Tsuga caroliniana

The Eastern Hemlock
Tsuga Canadensis

Style: *Tsuga canadensis* is a beautiful American evergreen tree, reaching a height of one hundred feet or more and a trunk width of four feet. **Leaves:** Needles are linear, dark green, and very finely toothed, from a quarter to two-thirds of an inch long, with two whitish bands beneath. **Flowers:** Inconspicuous. **Fruit:** An ovoid cone from one-half to three-quarters of an inch long. **Zone:** 3. **Uses:** Both in the garden and in the landscape, hemlocks are truly impressive trees. **Culture:** Do best in a cool, moist acid soil in full sun or some high, open shade. Shallow roots make them easy to transplant and fast growing. Can be sheared for a formal hedge. Not good in hot climates.

One or two small evergreens, especially hemlocks, standing gracefully on the brink of the rill, contrasting by their green with the surrounding deciduous trees when they have lost their leaves, and thus enlivening the scene and betraying their attachment to the water. It would be no more pleasing to me if the stream were a mile wide and the hemlocks five feet in diameter. I believe there is a harmony between the hemlock and the water which it overhangs not explainable. In the first place, its green is especially grateful to the eye the greater part of the year in any locality, and in the winter, but its verdure overhanging and shading the water, it concentrates in itself the beauty of all fluviatile trees. It loves to stand with its foot close to the water, its roots running over the rocks of the shore, and two or more on opposite sides of a brook make the most beautiful frame to a water scape, especially in deciduous woods, where the light is somber and not too glaring. It makes the more complete frame because its branches, particularly in young specimens such as I am thinking of, spring from so near the ground, and it makes so dense a mass of verdure. There are many larger hemlocks covering the steep side-hill forming the bank of the Assabet, where they are at every angle over the water. Some are almost horizontally directed, and almost every year one falls in and is washed away. The place is known as the "leaning Hemlocks." —April 1, 1852

HEMLOCKS ARE THE GLORY TREES OF THE CONIFEROUS WOODS. IN THOREAU'S Garden eastern hemlocks would carpet an area large enough to make an extensive woodland. This woods would include a swift-moving mountain stream. Even before Thoreau, hemlocks were considered elegant additions to a wooded landscape or arboretum.

Dr. Christopher Witt of Germantown, Pennsylvania, is thought to have established the first botanical garden in the colonies. He numbered among his good friends Peter Collinson, a Quaker linen draper of London and great garden enthusiast. Sometime before 1730, Witt sent some hemlocks "or small firs" to London, and Collinson planted them in his garden at Perkham in Surrey. In 1749, Collinson's collection, including the hemlocks, was moved to Mill Hill at Hendon, some eight miles northwest of London, an endeavor that took two years. Mill Hill became a boarding school for boys some two hundred years later, at which time the Witt hemlock was still growing. Measurements made in 1835 showed the tree to have two trunks, each a foot in diameter and about fifty feet high. In a 1932 letter to Charles F. Jenkins, the curator and founder of the Hemlock Arboretum at "Far Country" in Germantown, Major N. G. Brett-James, author of the life of Collinson, wrote, "The hemlock spruce is still in good health and is not changed in size from when Dr. H. Harris measured it in my company for Dr. Hingston Fox in 1923, and so it is almost exactly the same as in 1835. It's undoubtedly the oldest *Tsuga canadensis* growing in Great Britain." Such fidelity to a tree shows how much hemlocks are admired by both the garden and arboretum communities.

Barring future discoveries, there are fourteen hemlock species of which ten are Asiatic and two native to the Pacific states and adjacent Canada, one extending north to Alaska. Linnaeus included hemlock with the pines and in 1763 labeled it *Pinus canadensis*. In 1796, Michaux moved the hemlock to the firs, calling it *Picea canadensis*. In 1847, the Austrian botanist Stephen Ladislaus Endlicher first used *Tsuga*, the Japanese word for the hemlock. Because writing was introduced to Japan from China, some scholars believe that the Japanese word for the tree came from the Chinese character that means "tree with hanging branches"—an accurate description. Other specialists think the word *tsuga*, which in Japanese means "tree mother," was already in the Japanese language. In 1855, French botanist Elie Abel Carriere put all hemlocks into a separate family group under the generic name *Tsuga*. So in the tradition of botanical terminology, a great North American tree bears a Japanese name, which could be originally Chinese, conferred by an Austrian, confirmed by a Frenchman, and now accepted around the world.

Thoreau first mentioned the hemlock in 1851, when he called the tree a hemlock spruce, using the scientific name *Abies canadensis*, and the French Canadian term *pérusse*. He pointed out that the wood was used in Maine for threshing floors because it resists indentation.

> *I know of some memorable [trees] worth walking many miles to see. These little cheerful hemlocks,—the lisp of chickadees seems to come from them now,—each standing with its foot on the very edge of the stream, reaching sometimes part way over its channel, and here and there one has lightly stepped across. These evergreens are plainly as much for the shelter of birds as for anything else. The fallen leaves are so thick they almost fill the bed of the stream and choke it.* —November 4, 1851

Thoreau made a number of entries in the journal that concerned the lovely shape of the hemlock.

The lower branches of the hemlock point down, and even trail on the ground, the whole tree making a perfect canopy.
                                        —December 17, 1851

Some of the hemlock twigs, especially those that hang low about the trunks, broad, flat, and triangular like fans, edged with the recent yellowish green leaves about an inch deep, are very handsome and rich, shaped, the whole, like a fan or reticule, a foot base by eight or nine inches altitude. So many rich green drooping fans edged with yellowish hanging about the trunk.   —June 26, 1852

In three entries penned in spring, Thoreau notes how he was charmed by the look of the new growth on the eastern hemlock.

The hemlocks, whose fresh light green shoots have not grown half an inch or an inch, spotting the trees, contrasting with the dark green of last year's foliage, the fan-like sprays looking like bead bags.   —June 5, 1853

The hemlock woods, their fan-like sprays edged or spotted with short yellowish-green shoots, tier above tier, shelf above shelf, look like a cool bazaar of rich embroidered goods. How dense their shade, dark and cool beneath them as in a cellar! No plants grow there, but the ground is covered with fine red leaves. It is oftenest on a side-hill they grow.
                                        —June 6, 1853

Beautiful the hemlock-fans, now broad at the ends of the lower branches, which slant down, seen in the shade against the dark hillside. Such is the contrast of the very light green just put forth on their edges with the old very dark, I feast my eyes on it.   —June 6, 1854

The winter is also a great season to view hemlocks.

How snug and warm the hemlock looks in the winter! . . .
There is a tendency in the limbs to arrange themselves ray-
wise about a point one third from the base to the top. What
singular regularity in the outline of a tree!
                                                    —*December 14, 1855*

In one of his most lyrical descriptions, he mentions the beauty of the eastern hemlock coated with snow.

This forenoon I walk up the Assabet to see it. The hemlocks
are perhaps a richer sight than any tree,—such Christmas
trees, thus sugared, as were never seen. On [sic] side you see
more or less greenness, but when you stand due north they are
unexpectedly white and rich, so beautifully still, and when you
look under them you see some great rock, or rocks, all hoary
with the same, and a finer frost on the very dead hemlock
twigs there and on hanging roots and twigs, quite like the
cobwebs in a grist-mill covered with meal,—and it implies a
stillness like that; or it is like the lightest down glued on. The
birch, from its outline and its numerous twigs, is also one of
the prettiest trees in this dress.   —*January 13, 1859*

Beyond its aesthetic value, hemlocks are a must for those interested in gardening for wildlife. Thoreau describes both birds and squirrels taking advantage of hemlock cones.

Under the hill, on the southeast side of R. W. E.'s lot, where
the hemlock stands, I see many tracks of squirrels. The dark,
thick green of the hemlock (amid the pines) seems to attract
them as a cover. The snow under the hemlock is strewn with
the scales of cones, which they (and perhaps birds?) have
stripped off, and some of its little winged seeds. It is pleasant
to see the tracks of these squirrels (I am not sure whether
they are red or gray or both, for I see none) leading straight
from the base of one tree to that of another, thus leaving

*untrodden triangles, squares, and polygons of every form,
bounded by much trodden highways.* —December 7, 1859

*The snow and ice under the hemlocks is strewn with cones and
seeds and tracked with birds and squirrels. What a bountiful
supply of winter food is here provided for them! No sooner
has fresh snow fallen and covered up the old crop than down
comes a new supply all the more distinct on the spotless snow.
Here comes a little flock of chickadees, attracted by me as
usual, and perching close by boldly; then descending to the
snow and ice, I see them pick up the hemlock seed which lies
all around them. Occasionally they take one to a twig and
hammer at it there under their claws, perhaps to separate it
from the wing, or even the shell.* —January 19, 1860

The eastern hemlock once covered many acres in the mountains of New England and New York, spilling over into Pennsylvania, north through Canada to Nova Scotia, west to Minnesota,
and south along the Appalachians to the north of Alabama.

"Ah, that beautiful tree," said Thoreau, "with its green canopy,
under which little grows, not exciting the cupidity of the carpen-
ter, whose use most men have not discovered!"

Hemlocks were ignored for their timber, because the knots are
rock hard, and they quickly dulled old-fashioned equipment. But
when tannin was discovered in the bark, a gigantic tanning industry arose around the virgin hemlock forests. The boots of Civil War
troops were made supple with the trees from the Catskill Mountains. Hemlock groves were felled by greed until the Germans discovered a substitute tanning agent. By the end of the nineteenth
century, all the virgin hemlocks were gone and the industry died
on its feet.

Growing hemlock seedlings that you find on the forest floor
can be a fascinating hobby. Since a single tree produces numerous
seedlings, the ground that supports a hemlock grove will be covered with plants in various stages of growth. These little trees will

exhibit a great many variations in color, size of the needle, and the general shape of the tree itself. All that is needed is a sharp eye to pick out the most unusual and a shovel to move it to a better spot. If left to mature on their home ground, the mutants usually die out, because they cannot compete with their larger (and more normal) brethren for light, water, and soil nutrients. Hemlocks require an acid soil. During times of drought, the needles will turn yellow and fall. If this happens, immediately give the trees a good soaking and they will recover.

Hemlock seedlings are patient. These little trees will remain small for decades, shadowed by the mature trees above them. Then when a big tree dies or falls in a storm, nearby seedlings will suddenly shoot up, competing for the increased light provided by the fallen giant.

The Museum at the Royal Botanical Garden at Kew has a sample of bread made from the inner bark of the California mountain hemlock, *Tsuga mertensiana,* dating to 1793. The explorer Alexander Mackenzie, for whom the Mackenzie River in Oregon is named, received the bread as a gift from a Pacific Northwest Indian tribe, who considered it a great delicacy. Outside of casual mention of hemlock tea being used by lumbermen when no other drink was available, the bread is the only instance I've found of the tree being used as food.

In northern Scandinavia, Linnaeus once found large numbers of reindeer dying from a mysterious cause. He discovered they were eating cowbane (*Cicuta maculata*), a first cousin of poison hemlock (*Conium maculatum*). A concoction made from the leaves and roots of this last plant is thought to have been the fatal drink that ended the life of Socrates. Because the spreading branches of *Tsuga canadensis* resemble the highly pinnate leaves of *Conium,* early botanists confused the plants.

The American Indians also made a tea from the new needles of the Canadian hemlock and used it for kidney ailments. They added leafy branches to steam baths to treat rheumatism, colds, and coughs, and to induce sweating. The inner bark was steeped for a tea used to treat colds, diarrhea, fevers, coughs, scurvy, and various stomach problems. Because of its high tannin content, the bark is very astringent, and solutions of it were used to stop bleeding.

There are over two hundred registered cultivars of the eastern hemlock. Among my favorites are the following.

Jordan Jack describes 'Bennett', named in honor of his wife, as an eye-catching, low-growing hemlock that forms a natural weeping shrub with fine, light green foliage. It can be used in a large pot or planter on the terrace, eventually reaching a width of four feet and a height of three. 'Cappy's Choice' is a compact, weeping hemlock whose new growth is a soft, golden chartreuse that turns light green as summer progresses. 'Cole's Prostrate', sometimes known as Cole's prostrate hemlock, spills over rocks like water, following every contour. It shuns direct sunlight and prefers a moist soil. If staked, in a few years it will form a short trunk, with a cascade of weeping branches. 'Curley' has tightly spaced curled needles. 'Gentsch White' starts out the new growing season with distinct silver-white tips on its branches. 'Jervis' is a true dwarf that eventually forms an irregular pyramid about eighteen inches high. 'Minuta' must be the smallest hemlock on record. With five years' growth, these little plants will be four inches high, reaching ten inches in ten years. 'Pendula' is a weeping hemlock that must be staked and tied upright for a few years to get the marvelous rounded weeping form. In ten years the plant will be two feet high and four feet wide.

The Carolina Hemlock
Tsuga caroliniana

THOREAU WAS UNFAMILIAR with the Carolina hemlock, but I mention it here because of its beauty and usefulness in the garden. In his monumental book on conifers, *The Cultivated Conifers in North America* (New York: The Macmillan Company, 1933), Liberty Hyde Bailey writes that the Carolina hemlock is "generally hardy in New England and a very desirable tree," and Bailey never gave out compliments to plants unless they really deserved them.

In *Growing & Propagating Showy Native Woody Plants* (Chapel Hill: University of North Carolina Press, 1992), Richard E. Bir points out that the eastern hemlock has a relatively shallow but very aggressive root system that takes advantage of most garden situations, resulting in neighboring plants needing special attention. "If a gardener chooses Carolina hemlock, instead, competition will be greatly reduced while the visual effect will be much the same. Why? Carolina hemlock is a tap-rooted plant: most of its roots will grow down rather than out."

Julia Ellen Rogers, writing in *The Tree Book* (New York: Doubleday, Page & Company, 1914), claimed that the Carolina hemlock "has found favor with landscape gardeners, because it is more graceful

> **Style:** Even more beautiful than the eastern hemlock but not as large, usually reaching only seventy feet. **Leaves:** Needles are linear, dark green and glossy above, with white bands beneath, one-third to three-quarters of an inch long. **Flowers:** Inconspicuous. **Fruit:** Cones are oblong, one to one and a half inches long. **Zone:** 6. **Uses:** A beautiful landscape and garden tree, as well as an effective hedge. **Culture:** Tolerant of most conditions but does best in an average, acid soil in full sun or some high, open shade. Tap-rooted, so slower growing for the first ten years but more drought tolerant than the eastern. Can be sheared as a formal hedge. Not good in hot climates.

though more compact than the Eastern hemlock. It is a hardy, handsome tree in New England parks, and its popularity is growing."

Finally, William Chambers Coker and Henry Roland Totten, the authors of *Trees of the Southeastern States* (Chapel Hill: University of North Carolina Press, 1934), described the Carolina hemlock as being discovered on Table Mountain, Pickens County, South Carolina, in 1837 by Dr. L. R. Gibbes, who gave it the scientific name of *Pinus laxa*. It wasn't until twenty-five years later, long after Thoreau's death, that George Engelmann properly named the tree. "The Carolina hemlock," they wrote, "is a very beautiful tree in cultivation, perhaps the handsomest of any eastern American conifer."

For smaller gardens, two beautiful cultivars of the Carolina hemlock are available. *Tsuga caroliniana* 'Compacta' is a dwarf cultivar, very broad, slow growing, and densely branched. 'Labar Weeping' is a slow-growing, prostrate form that cascades over rocks; if staked it becomes a beautiful weeper.

THOREAU'S FERN BED

As when Antaeus touched the earth, so when the mountaineer
scents the fern, he bounds up like a chamois, or mountain
goat, with renewed strength. There is no French perfumery
about it. It has not been tampered with by any perfumer to
their majesties. It is the fragrance of those plants whose
impressions we see on our coal. Beware of the cultivation
that eradicates it.   —*September 24, 1859*

Antaeus was the son of Poseidon, the god who protected all waters of the Earth, and Gaea, the Earth goddess. He was a mighty wrestler with invincible strength, as long as he retained contact with his mother Earth. Every stranger that entered Libya had to wrestle with Antaeus, and the loser was put to death. Hercules found that he couldn't best this mighty gatekeeper no matter how hard he tried. Then on a sudden inspiration—or possibly a secret communication from the gods—he lifted Antaeus into the air, whereupon Antaeus immediately lost his strength and Hercules crushed him to death.

Thoreau mentions ferns in his journals on dozens of occasions.

The delicate maidenhair fern forms a cup or dish, very deli-
cate and graceful. Beautiful, too, its glossy black stem and
wave-edged fruited leaflets. I hear the feeble plaintive note
of young bluebirds, just trying their wings or getting used to
them. Young robins peep.   —*June 13, 1852*

—the ferns of various species and in various stages, some
now in their most perfect and beautiful condition, com-
pletely unfolded, tender and delicate, but perfect in all their
details, far more than any lace work—the most elaborate
leaf we have.   —*May 25, 1853*

The Structure of Ferns

BEFORE WE PICK AMONG THOREAU'S FAVORITE FERNS, A FEW TERMS
should be defined.

Ferns are far older on the geologic timetable and were in existence long before the more sophisticated annuals, perennials, grasses, bushes, shrubs, and trees that came upon the earth to flower.

Ferns grow from rootstocks or, more properly, *rhizomes*. Usually covered with scales or hairs, these structures are perennial (although *Annogramma leptophylla,* a little fern discovered about one hundred years ago on the Channel Islands, is an annual).

The *stalk* (preferred to the word *stem,* which is usually used for flowering plants) supports the leaf and is often flat or concave in front, rounded in back, and covered with hairs or scales, especially when the stalks are young.

Fern leaves are also called *fronds* or *blades.* The species are differentiated by the characters of the leaves, the shapes of which vary from simple to compound, with many divisions. Some ferns have two kinds of leaves. Sterile leaves support photosynthesis, whereas the fertile leaves bear the spores.

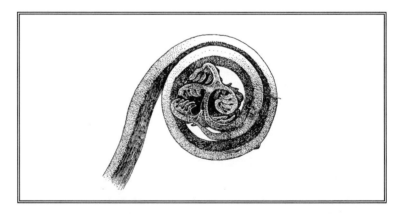

The word *fiddlehead* refers to the young, unfurling leaves of the true ferns. In the spring the new leaves are tightly coiled and look like the head of a violin or the top of a bishop's crosier. Many fiddleheads are covered with dense woolly scales for added protection against late spring freezes.

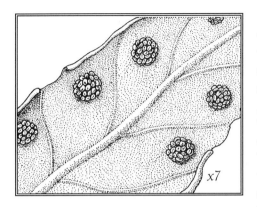

In the summertime, tiny greenish and usually rounded specks appear on the undersides of fern leaves, and gardeners may fear that the ferns are diseased or infested with bugs. But these specks soon turn into dark brown spots called *sori,* from the Greek word for heaps. These sori, or fruit dots (I think much the better term), are tiny masses of spore cases, or *sporangia,* which contain the fern's spores.

The spores are like seeds, but the life cycle of a fern is more complex than that of a flowering plant. When a spore finds a warm, damp place, it develops into a *prothallus,* a structure that begins life as one cell but soon grows into a heart-shaped, flat

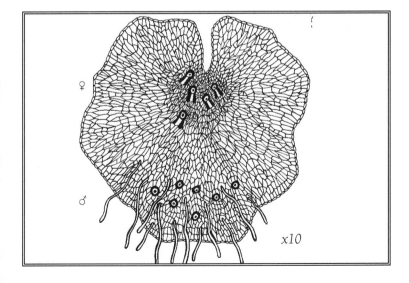

structure about one-quarter of an inch wide with tiny roots on its lower surface.

Soon both egg-containing organs called *archegonia* and sperm-producing organs called *antheridia* appear on the underside of the prothallus, and when mature, the antheridia release sperm that swim through the tiniest bit of moisture to the archegonia and fertilize the eggs inside. When that occurs, a true fern begins to grow. Imagine all this going on in the fern bed.

The Lady Fern
Athyrium Filix-femina

Style: The lady fern is showy and graceful with finely cut leaves. **Stalk:** Usually shorter than the blade and flat or grooved in the front, smooth, and green. **Leaves:** Deciduous, about thirty inches tall and about ten inches wide, lance shaped with a pointed tip, growing in a circular cluster; twenty-four pairs of usually not-opposite leaflets are cut again into about twelve pairs of subleaflets. **Fruit dots:** Horseshoe shaped, of a dark brown. **Uses:** A most beautiful fern for the fern garden, preferring moist soil in partial shade.

ON SEPTEMBER 30, 1859, THE LADY FERN WAS, ACCORDING TO THOREAU, "decaying, maybe a little later than the dicksonia,—the largish fern with long, narrow pinnules deeply cut and toothed, and reniform [kidney-shaped] fruit-dots." He identifies it as *Asplenium Filix-foemina,* a name that eventually gave way to *Athyrium Filix-femina. Athyrium,* which comes from the Greek *athyro,* to sport, refers to the many shapes of the fruit dots in this particular genus.

In *Waverly,* Sir Walter Scott pays the lady fern the compliment of mentioning it by name:

> Where the copse wood is the greenest,
> Where the fountain glistens sheenest,
> Where the morning dew lies longest,
> There the Lady Fern grows strongest.

And that's not bad growing advice when it comes to siting this fern.

In July 1857, Thoreau noted an *Aspidium noveboracense* at Corner Spring that had not yet browned from the summer heat.

> . . . *also* Aspidium Noveboracense *with lunar-shaped fruit, not yet brown.* —*July 15, 1857*

Six days earlier, while walking at Blister Spring swamp, he saw several species of ferns.

> Aspidium Noveboracense, *more than half of it turned white. Also some dicksonia is about equally white. These especially are the white ones. There is another, largish, and more generally decayed than either of these, with large serrated segments, rather far apart,—perhaps the* Asplenium Filix-foemina? *The first may be called the white fern,—with rather small entirish and flat segments close together. In shade is the laboratory of white. Color is produced in the sun. The cinnamon ferns are all a decaying brown there.*

*The sober brown colors of those ferns are in harmony with
the twilight of the swamp. The terminal shield fern and the
Aspidium spinulosum (?) are still fresh and green, the first
as much as the polypody.*   *—July 9, 1857*

The species name *Filix-femina* harks back to the Greeks and
Romans who, while very sophisticated about animal sex, were
completely at sea when it came to plants. If two plants were very
similar, they would simply call the smaller female and the larger
male. For hundreds of years confusion reigned over male fern
(*Dryopteris Filix-mas*), female or lady fern, and bracken or brake
(*Pteridium aquilinum*). The situation was summed up in 1548 by
William Turner: "*Felix* is called in Greek *Pteris*, in English a fern or
a brake. There are two kinds of brakes. The one kind is called in
Latin *Filix mascula* and in Greek *Pteris*. The second kind is called
in Greek *Thelypteris*, in Latin *Filix femina*, that is the common fern
or brake, which the Northern men call a bracken."

Lady fern has a long history of medicinal use, and the American
Indians used a root tea as a diuretic and to stop childbirth pains.

The Dryopteris Ferns

*In the Lee farm swamp, by the old Sam Barrett mill site, I
see two kinds of ferns still green and much in fruit, apparently the* Aspidium spinulosum *(?) and* cristatum *(?).
They are also common in other swamps now. They are quite
fresh in those cold and wet places and almost flattened down
now. The atmosphere of the house is less congenial to them.
In the summer you might not have noticed them. Now they
are conspicuous amid the withered leaves. You are inclined
to approach and raise each frond in succession, moist, trembling, fragile greenness. They linger thus in all moist
clammy swamps under the bare maples and grape-vines
and witch-hazels, and about each trickling spring which is
half choked with fallen leaves. What makes this persistent*

vitality, invulnerable to frost and wet? Why were these spared when the brakes and osmundas were stricken down? They stay as if to keep up the spirits of the cold-blooded frogs which have not yet gone into the mud; that the summer may die with decent and graceful moderation, gradually. Is not the water of the spring improved by their presence? They fall back and droop here and there, like the plumes of de-parting summer,—of the departing year. Even in them I feel an argument for immortality. How valuable they are (with the lycopodiums) for cheerfulness. Greenness at the end of the year, after the fall of the leaf, as in a hale old age. To my eyes they are tall and noble as palm groves, and always some forest nobleness seems to have its haunt under their umbrage. Each such green tuft of ferns is a grove where some nobility dwells and walks. All that was immortal in the swamp's heritage seems here crowded into smaller com-pass,—the concentrated greenness of the swamp. How dear they must be to the chickadee and the rabbit!

—*October 30, 1857*

THE NAME DRYOPTERIS IS FROM THE GREEK DRYS, OR OAK, AND PTERIS, OR fern. The majority of the species in this genus are usually found in oak woods. In Thoreau's day they were in the genus *Aspidium* (Greek for "little shield"). The spinulose woodfern, Thoreau's *Aspidium spinulosum,* is now *Dryopteris spinulosa,* and the crested fern, *Aspidium cristatum,* is now *Dryopteris cristata.*

The Crested or Prickly-toothed Shield Fern
Dryopteris cristata

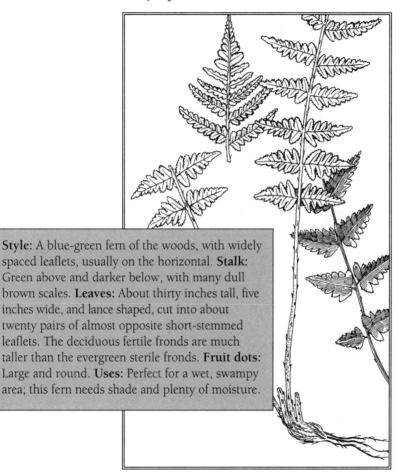

Style: A blue-green fern of the woods, with widely spaced leaflets, usually on the horizontal. **Stalk:** Green above and darker below, with many dull brown scales. **Leaves:** About thirty inches tall, five inches wide, and lance shaped, cut into about twenty pairs of almost opposite short-stemmed leaflets. The deciduous fertile fronds are much taller than the evergreen sterile fronds. **Fruit dots:** Large and round. **Uses:** Perfect for a wet, swampy area; this fern needs shade and plenty of moisture.

DRYOPTERIS CRISTATA AND D. SPINULOSA ARE THE FERNS KNOWN AS "FANCY ferns" that florists once gathered from northeastern woods. This practice led to a rapid decline in the population of these ferns. *D. cristata* is often found growing from decaying tree trunks.

The Spinulose Woodfern
Dryopteris spinulosa

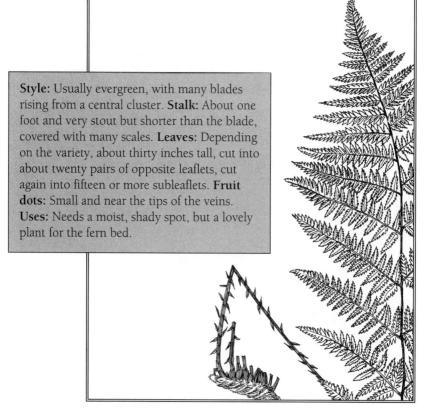

Style: Usually evergreen, with many blades rising from a central cluster. **Stalk:** About one foot and very stout but shorter than the blade, covered with many scales. **Leaves:** Depending on the variety, about thirty inches tall, cut into about twenty pairs of opposite leaflets, cut again into fifteen or more subleaflets. **Fruit dots:** Small and near the tips of the veins. **Uses:** Needs a moist, shady spot, but a lovely plant for the fern bed.

Ever since the unusually early and severe frost of the 16th, the evergreen ferns have been growing more and more distinct amid the fading and decaying and withering ones, and the sight of those suggests a cooler season. They are greener than ever, by contrast.... The most decidedly evergreen are the ... Aspidium spinulosum ...   —*September 30, 1859*

The Hay-scented or Boulder Fern
Dennstaedtia punctilobula

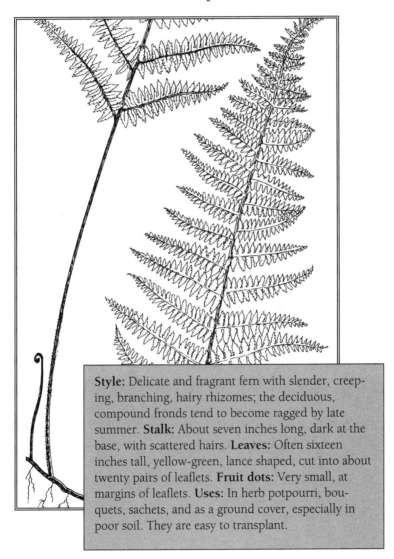

Style: Delicate and fragrant fern with slender, creeping, branching, hairy rhizomes; the deciduous, compound fronds tend to become ragged by late summer. **Stalk:** About seven inches long, dark at the base, with scattered hairs. **Leaves:** Often sixteen inches tall, yellow-green, lance shaped, cut into about twenty pairs of leaflets. **Fruit dots:** Very small, at margins of leaflets. **Uses:** In herb potpourri, bouquets, sachets, and as a ground cover, especially in poor soil. They are easy to transplant.

Going along this old Carlisle road,—road for walkers, for berry-pickers, and no more worldly travelers; . . . not for the sheriff nor butcher nor the baker's jingling cart; road where all wild things and fruits abound, where there are countless rocks to jar those who venture there in wagons . . . as I was going along there, I perceived the grateful scent of the dicksonia fern, now partly decayed, and it reminds me of all up-country with its springy mountainsides and unexhausted vigor. Is there an essence of dicksonia fern, I wonder?

—September 24, 1859

THOREAU CALLED THE HAY-SCENTED FERN DICKSONIA (*DICKSONIA punctilobula*), named for James Dickson, a British nurseryman and botanist. The genus is now *Dennstaedtia*, named for August Wilhelm Dennstedt, a German botanist of the early nineteenth century.

Growing equally well in shade or full sun in the Northeast, the hay-scented fern prospers not only along Thoreau's Carlisle road but also in places of almost pure rock, giving rise to its other common name of boulder fern. In her 1899 book, *How to Know the Ferns*, Frances Theodora Parsons writes that this fern often grows "along the roadsides [forming] great masses of feathery foliage, tempting the weary pedestrian or bicycler to fling himself upon a couch sufficiently soft and luxurious in appearance to satisfy a Sybarite." She describes a memorably hot August afternoon when, on a trip over an unused mountain road, her party succumbed to weariness. The group gathered armloads of fern fronds for a night's rest, but Ms. Parsons's night was less than restful: "I must frankly own that I never slept on so hard a bed."

In the lowest part of the road the dicksonia by the wall-sides is more than half frost-bitten and withered,—a sober Quaker-color, brown crepe!—though not so tender or early

[?] as the cinnamon fern; but soon rise to where they are more yellow and green, and so my route is varied. On the higher places there are very handsome tufts of it, all yellowish outside and green within. The sweet fragrance of decay!
                                        —September 24, 1859

Waning sunlight and cooler nights apparently prime the hay-scented fern for the coming demise of its upper parts. As early as late September in the mountains around Asheville, the fronds begin their color decline from light green to pale green to light tan and often to pure white as the season marches on to winter.

Faded white ferns now at Saw Mill Brook. —October 24, 1855

When I wade through by narrow cow-paths, it is as if I had strayed into an ancient and decayed herb-garden. Proper for old ladies to scent their handkerchiefs with. Nature perfumes her garments with this essence now especially. She gives it to those who go a-barberrying and on dank autumnal walks. The essence of this as well as of new-mown hay, surely! The very scent of it, if you have a decayed frond in your chamber, will take you up country in a twinkling. You would think you had gone after the cows there, or were lost on the mountains.   *—September 24, 1859*

The fragrance is attributable to the chemical coumarin, which is contained within glandular hairs that sprout from the leaflets. Coumarin, a white crystalline substance with a vanillalike odor, is found in many plants, including American sweet grass (*Hierochloe odorata*), which American Indians used both as a flavoring and to weave into baskets and mats. Coumarin also accounts for the fragrance of zubrowka, a Russian vodka with three or four blades of

Russian buffalo grass (*H. australis*) added to a quart of the spirit. The sweet odor of the grass infuses this clear liquor.

Thoreau, however, wasn't smelling vodka. When writing about the hay-scented fern, Thoreau notes that "this is the scent of the Silurian Period precisely, and a modern beau may scent his handkerchief with it."

Thoreau probably should have chosen the much later Jurassic Period, where the earliest fossils of the *Dennstaedtia* have been found.

The Sensitive or Bead Fern
Onoclea sensibilis

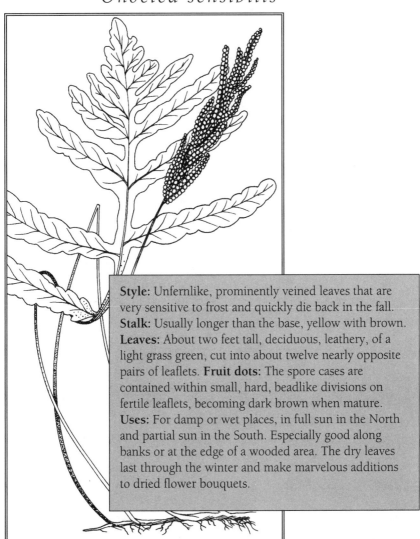

Style: Unfernlike, prominently veined leaves that are very sensitive to frost and quickly die back in the fall. **Stalk:** Usually longer than the base, yellow with brown. **Leaves:** About two feet tall, deciduous, leathery, of a light grass green, cut into about twelve nearly opposite pairs of leaflets. **Fruit dots:** The spore cases are contained within small, hard, beadlike divisions on fertile leaflets, becoming dark brown when mature. **Uses:** For damp or wet places, in full sun in the North and partial sun in the South. Especially good along banks or at the edge of a wooded area. The dry leaves last through the winter and make marvelous additions to dried flower bouquets.

> *The fertile fruit-stems of the sensitive fern, by the side of the*
> *Flint's Pond path, more than a foot high, are a rich ornament*
> *to the ground,—brown, four or five inches long, and turned to*
> *one side, contrasting with the lighter rachis (?)*
> —*April 25, 1854*

THOREAU QUESTIONS THE USE OF THE WORD RACHIS, WHICH MEANS THE axis of a compound leaf, but even though the spore cases of the sensitive fern are indeed strange when compared with other ferns, they begin as parts of a fertile leaf.

The sensitive fern belongs to a one-species genus native to the north temperate regions of both hemispheres. Descriptions of the plant usually point out its weedy tendency and the rough and tumble aspect of its leaves, which in no way resemble the fronds of typical ferns.

First found in Virginia, the sensitive fern was named in 1753, about one hundred years before Thoreau commented on it in his journal. The scientific name *Onoclea* comes from *onos*, vessel, and *kleio*, to close, in reference to the closely rolled fertile fronds. This fern is *dimorphic*, a word meaning "two forms." For example, in some plants, like English ivy (*Hedera helix*), there is a juvenile form that is entirely different from the mature form of the plant. In sensitive ferns, the spore cases on the fertile leaflets look like the beadwork on Indian moccasins.

> *How handsome now the fertile fronds of the sensitive fern,*
> *standing up a foot or more on the sides of causeways, the*
> *neat pale-brown stipe clothed with rich dark-brown fruit at*
> *top, —the pinnae on one side and slightly curved, —"a one*
> *sided spike or raceme," —still full of seed! They look quite*
> *fresh though dry and rigid.* —*January 9, 1855*

Why the common name sensitive when dealing with a fern that is hardy to Zone 3? On September 5, 1856, one Mr. Charles

Frost at Brattleboro showed Thoreau some wildflowers and spoke of the fragrance of the hay-scented fern "and the sensitiveness of the sensitive fern. If you take a tender plant by the stem, the warmth of your hand will cause the leaves to curl." I've never tried it, but it is a fact that the slightest touch of frost will cause the leaves to brown quickly and curl up with the speed of a vampire touched by sunlight.

In *obtusilobata* the sterile fronds look like a wet bird feather and sometimes produce a small crop of spores, usually after the plant has been mowed or injured in some way.

The Cinnamon Fern
Osmunda cinnamomea

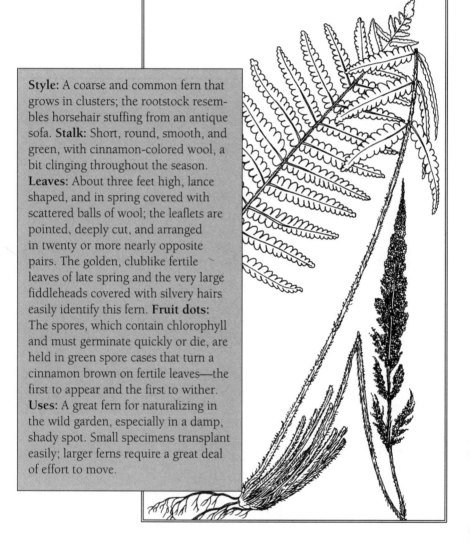

Style: A coarse and common fern that grows in clusters; the rootstock resembles horsehair stuffing from an antique sofa. **Stalk:** Short, round, smooth, and green, with cinnamon-colored wool, a bit clinging throughout the season. **Leaves:** About three feet high, lance shaped, and in spring covered with scattered balls of wool; the leaflets are pointed, deeply cut, and arranged in twenty or more nearly opposite pairs. The golden, clublike fertile leaves of late spring and the very large fiddleheads covered with silvery hairs easily identify this fern. **Fruit dots:** The spores, which contain chlorophyll and must germinate quickly or die, are held in green spore cases that turn a cinnamon brown on fertile leaves—the first to appear and the first to wither. **Uses:** A great fern for naturalizing in the wild garden, especially in a damp, shady spot. Small specimens transplant easily; larger ferns require a great deal of effort to move.

The ferns invested with rusty wool have pushed up eight or ten inches and show some of the green leaf. The fertile fronds are at first a dark green, later a cinnamon-brown and soon encircled by a tall crown of sterile fronds. They are a true thing of beauty when well-planted and provided with plenty of water but in a dry spot, they soon look forlorn.

—May 1854

THE GENUS *OSMUNDA* IS SAID TO BE NAMED AFTER OSMUNDER, THE SAXON name of Thor. The original specimens used to identify this plant came from Maryland in 1753. The roots of the osmunda ferns have been gathered for many years to produce a tough growing medium for orchids that provides a good holdfast for their roots and needed nutrients as it decays. But increased demand has led to higher prices, and it's now scare and expensive.

Cinnamon ferns prefer damp or wet locations and are especially fond of growing in swamps, where they impart a tropical look to the landscape, even in New England. This fern will grow in a lot of sun even in the South, but it always achieves a better form in a shaded location.

The Common Polypody
Polypodium virginianum

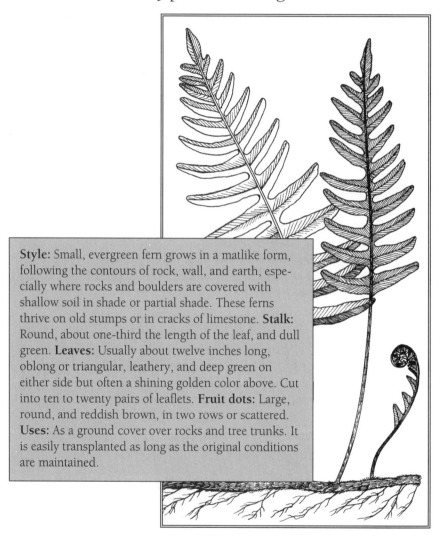

Style: Small, evergreen fern grows in a matlike form, following the contours of rock, wall, and earth, especially where rocks and boulders are covered with shallow soil in shade or partial shade. These ferns thrive on old stumps or in cracks of limestone. **Stalk:** Round, about one-third the length of the leaf, and dull green. **Leaves:** Usually about twelve inches long, oblong or triangular, leathery, and deep green on either side but often a shining golden color above. Cut into ten to twenty pairs of leaflets. **Fruit dots:** Large, round, and reddish brown, in two rows or scattered. **Uses:** As a ground cover over rocks and tree trunks. It is easily transplanted as long as the original conditions are maintained.

*Why is not this form copied by our sculptors instead of the
foreign acanthus leaves? How fit for a tuft about the base of
a column! The sight of this unwithering green leaf excites me
like red at some seasons. Are not woodfrogs the philosophers
who frequent such groves? Methinks I imbibe a cool, composed, frog-like philosophy when I behold them.*
—*November 2, 1857*

THE GENUS NAME *POLYPODIUM* MEANS "MANY FEET" AND REFERS TO THE
traces of the many stalks on old rhizomes. A large genus, the polypodys include many epiphytic tropical ferns.

The polypodys are common in Europe, the British Isles, and
most of the United States. Thoreau referred to the "fresh and
cheerful communities" of the polypody in early spring.

The Canadian French call the common polypody *tripe de
roche,* referring to the rich and velvety growth that grows over
rocks and boulders. Other common names include moss fern, oak
fern, rock-cap fern, snake fern, stone fern, wall fern, and poly-
pody-of-the-oak.

*The form of the polypody is strangely interesting, it is even
outlandish. Some forms, though common in our midst, are
thus perennially foreign as the growths of other latitudes;
there being a greater interval between us and their kind
than usual. We all feel the ferns to be further from us . . .
[than] the roses and weeds, for instance. It needs no geology
nor botany to assure us of that. We feel it, and told them of
it first. The bare outline of the polypody thrills me strangely.
It is a strange type which I cannot read. It only piques me.
Simple as it is, it is as strange as an Oriental character. It is
quite independent of my race, and of the Indian, and all
mankind. It is a fabulous, mythological form, such as prevailed
when the earth and air and water were inhabited by those
extinct fossil creatures that we find.*   —*November 2, 1857*

The Druids held the oak in high esteem and believed that anything that grew on oak, like the polypody, would inherit the oak's
magic. The American Indians used a polypody root tea to treat
hives and sore throats, and it was once thought to be especially
valuable in the treatment of both lung and liver disease. The roots
contain the sugars fructose, glucose, and sucrose, plus a winter-
green flavoring producing a sweetish taste that quickly becomes
nauseating. Then, too, the presence in the roots of up to two per-
cent "insect regulating hormones" and resins that are active against
worms puts ingestion of this plant on the danger list.

Long before Thoreau extolled the beauties of polypody, Izaak
Walton gave this advice in *The Compleat Angler:* "Take the stinking
oil drawn out of polypody . . . mix with turpentine and hive honey,
and anoint your bait therewith."

For years the American polypody was called *Polypodium vulgare,* the scientific name of its European counterpart. For a time it
was known as *P. vulgare* var. *virginianum.* Now the American plant
is considered a separate species, *P. virginianum.* But just to compli-
cate matters, *P. virginianum* is really a complex of forms with different chromosome numbers: diploids, tetraploids, and their hybrid
triploids, each having two, four, and three sets of chromosomes,
respectively. Now, after additional research, it's been determined
that the diploid and the tetraploid forms are really separate species.
As a result, the tetraploids are called *P. virginianum,* and the diploids
P. appalachianum. The shape of the fronds is usually enough to
identify the various species and the hybrid form. According to the
American Fern Society, *P. appalachianum* is the more common fern,
at least in New York and Pennsylvania.

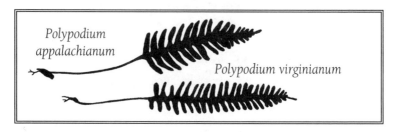

*Polypodium
appalachianum*

Polypodium virginianum

The New York Fern
Thelypteris noveboracensis

Style: A delicate but large medium green fern, the blades fading to tan, then almost white in early fall. **Stalk:** About eight inches long, smooth or slightly hairy. **Leaves:** About eighteen inches tall and about six inches wide, tapering up and down from the middle; the leaves are cut into about twenty usually opposite, stemless leaflets that are cut again into twenty or more pairs of rounded subleaflets. **Fruit dots:** Few and small near margins of the leaflets. **Uses:** Liking dry woods, the creeping rootstock hugs the ground and is very easy to transplant.

NAMED IN 1753, THE NEW YORK FERN RANGES FROM ONTARIO WEST TO Minnesota, then south to Arkansas and east to Georgia.

Thoreau called it the white fern, and it's often mistaken for the hay-scented fern because the leaves of both whiten as they die.

> *In Potter's maple swamp I see the (apparently) Aspidum Thelypteris (revolute segments) about half decaying or whitish, but later than the flower fern and the osmunda, which are almost entirely withered and brown there.*
> —*September 26, 1859*

Mixed in with other ferns and perennials, the soft tans of this fern's blades give a subtle contrast to the garden, something to take the edge off the more blatant colors of fall. Frances Parsons saw them "throng to the roadside, which is flanked by a tangled thicket of osmundas, wild roses, and elder bushes." Thoreau saw them in Potter's Maple Swamp, and we look forward to seeing them every year.